"In this book Anna Carter Florence goes on a wild rumpus invigorating God's people to be a repertory church searching for something true. Treating Scripture as a fridge full of promise rather than a ready-made meal waiting to be microwaved, Florence provides a recipe to enliven Scripture reading and performance in our lives. Her *Rehearsing Scripture* will renew your practice and awaken your imagination."

– **Samuel Wells**
author of *Incarnational Ministry* and *Learning to Dream Again*

"A fascinating and fruitful guide for reading and living out Scripture. If you believe that the Bible has something important to say but find that Bible studies are often tedious, repetitive, or confrontational, this book is for you. If you wish to hear the Bible anew, this book is for you. If you are part of a Bible study group that seems to have lost its original energy, this book is for you."

– **Justo L. González**
author of *A Brief History of Sunday: From the New Testament to the New Creation*

"Into this lively book Anna Carter Florence pours her experience as an outstanding preacher and teacher of preachers. Scripture is known in its performance. The test of my preaching is in its enactment in the lives of my congregation. Florence's love of and deep engagement with Scripture are infectious. Fresh insights are found here on every page."

– **William H. Willimon**
author of *Who Lynched Willie Earle? Preaching to Confront Racism*

"For any preachers who have glided blithely through a biblical text on the way to writing a sermon, Anna Carter Florence calls us to repent and to pay close attention to the text again. Under her guidance the biblical passage is transformed from a sermon pretext into a rich drama bursting with power. Verbs, flattened by hasty and inattentive readings, now loom as mountains of meaning, and characters, once hardly noticed stick figures, become animated, articulate, and forceful. As a result, preachers do not 'preach themselves.' Instead they point a trembling finger at the text, saying 'I can't wait to tell you what's happening in there!'"

– **Thomas G. Long**
author of *The Witness of Preaching* and
What Shall We Say? Evil, Suffering,
and the Crisis of Faith

Rehearsing Scripture

Discovering God's Word in Community

Anna Carter Florence

William B. Eerdmans Publishing Company
Grand Rapids, Michigan

Wm. B. Eerdmans Publishing Co.
2140 Oak Industrial Drive N.E., Grand Rapids, Michigan 49505
www.eerdmans.com

Published 2018
Printed in the United States of America

27 26 25 24 23 22 21 20 19 18   1 2 3 4 5 6 7 8 9 10

ISBN 978-0-8028-7412-2

Library of Congress Cataloging-in-Publication Data

Names: Florence, Anna Carter, author.
Title: Rehearsing scripture : discovering God's word in community / Anna Carter Florence.
Description: Grand Rapids : Eerdmans Publishing Co., 2018. | Includes bibliographical references and index.
Identifiers: LCCN 2018006909 | ISBN 9780802874122 (pbk. : alk. paper)
Subjects: LCSH: Bible—Hermeneutics. | Small groups.
Classification: LCC BS476 .F64 2018 | DDC 220.601—dc23
LC record available at https://lccn.loc.gov/2018006909

Contents

Part II
Encountering Scripture in the Repertory Church

Five More Tools for Rehearsing Scripture

Preface

The Day I Learned to Read (All Over Again)

My sophomore year of college, I signed up for a course called "Theater Studies," a class I knew nothing about and which I hoped would be a break in my schedule. The course description was a little vague: "a survey of theory and practice." I had no idea what that meant, but figured we would be reading plays by Shakespeare and watching films that featured famous British actors. It seemed like the kind of class a history major could breeze through without having to spend every night in the library—something I was already doing plenty of in my other classes. Besides, weren't plays more fun than textbooks? And twice as fast to read?

Well, yes. And then no. And then yes, again.

The "theory" component of the class turned out to be a series of Monday-afternoon lectures so dense that I needed a dictionary just to keep up. As my professor held forth on such baffling concepts as hermeneutics, semiotics, and performativity in Elizabethan drama (with words I could barely spell, let alone pronounce), I considered dropping the course, and judging from the looks on the other students' faces, I wasn't the only one. But the rest of the week was brilliant. We left the sleek lecture hall, trooped to the second floor of a dusty old building down the street, and moved our chairs into a circle for the "practice" part of the class. My professor stopped talking about the plays we were reading and set us loose with them. "Go rehearse a scene," he told us. "Come back when you've found something true, show us, and we'll see."

Come back when you've found something true. A whole new world opened up to me with that phrase and that year. I learned that lectures and theories and reference tools are important, but they can only take a reader so far. Some texts need to be practiced. We need to be set loose with them. We need to go and rehearse them, together, and to come back and show one another when we've found something true. And then, we'll see. We'll talk and rework what happened. And somehow, through a power that is never our own, we will see God, and so ourselves, more deeply and truly than we could ever do on our own.

Down the road, some years later, another world opened up. I realized that Scripture, too, is a text that needs to be practiced—and rehearsed. Scripture is meant to be studied and examined, but also encountered, and we do this work best when we do it together. Rehearsing is a way of encountering. It helps us find the script in Scripture: *our* script. And those encounters with Scripture are meant to be shared. It's an amazing thing, to find something true! I began to wonder: how can we encourage each other to read and rehearse the biblical text, and come back and show one another when we've found something true? How can we rehearse Scripture, in community, to discover God's Word?

This is a book that will show you how to do just that. It's designed to be used with groups, as an aid to breathe new life into your reading and interpretation of Scripture.

I wrote this book because I have a very odd job: I teach preaching, in a seminary, for people who are preparing to go out and *say something true* about Scripture. You might think this would entail a lot of talking, or teaching others how to talk, but it's mainly about reading—and not alone in a library. My students are already very good at that. What they need help with is learning to read in some new ways that will get them out of the library and into a practice room, with their chairs moved into a circle. Since they're already *studying* and *examining* the biblical text, they need space to *rehearse* and *encounter* it.

So I invite them to read Scripture in some new ways. Not alone: together. Not once: again and again. Not to explain or portray the text in some definitive version, but to find something true, alongside other true discoveries. It is reading as a community—and it forms community. And just like my Theater Studies class from long ago, it makes my students hungry for the text and for the joy of showing one another all that the text can say. Then we have plenty to talk about! We can't wait to come back and *say something true* about the God we've encountered in our reading.

We've learned something else, too. People who fundamentally disagree with one another can gather around Scripture in this way, and enjoy doing it! We can stop fighting about what the text means, and start listening to it, and to one another. We can find something *true* before we decide what's *right*. And then—best surprise of all—people whose views we never dreamed we might respect or value turn out to have perspectives on the text we come to treasure. When the world around us is crazy with conflict, rehearsing Scripture might just be the start of game-changing community. It has been for us. I hope it might be for you, too.

This Book in Your Hands

With this book, you and a group can begin a reading adventure that will help you dive into Scripture in some ways you never knew you could—or imagined would lead to the places it does. You may never have read the Bible in this way (or at all), but that's fine: everything you need to do it is already within you! The good news about rehearsing Scripture is that it doesn't require any special skills or expertise. It just takes a group of people who are eager to discover God's Word, and who are up for the adventure, with all of its joys and surprises.

This book will give you the tools you need to get ready and get started. Part I (chapters 1–6) deals with practical matters. What exactly is "reading and rehearsing Scripture," and why is it such an effective way for groups to enter the biblical text? How does it build community and bind us together? Can we really find a story we recognize—*a script in Scripture*—that will speak truth to our lives? If we imagined ourselves as a *repertory church* that's committed to reading and living the scripts in Scripture, could we then speak that truth to the world?

I'm drawing on the world of theater for much of this, so we'll be adapting dramatic ideas and practices for ordinary (that is, undramatic) people like us. We'll take a close look at the dynamic language of Scripture: the fact that it *moves* and asks us to move with it, to pay attention to the action words and what they tell us. We'll follow up on that, and learn to *read the verbs* in a biblical text—the most efficient way I know to dive into Scripture with depth and precision. Then we'll consider a host of helpful, often hilarious ways for a group to broaden its reading: questions to ask, rehearsal techniques to try, rules of fair play to keep things steady, and ways to move from reading to speaking. We'll practice each of these and apply them to a single text throughout all the chapters of Part I—Genesis 3:1-10, the story of the man and the woman and the serpent in the Garden of Eden—to see how the process works. Along the way, if you want more concrete details, you can turn to one of the five appendices in the back of the book; they offer specifics and directions you can adapt for your own group's needs.

In Part II (chapters 7-10), we turn from reading to speaking, with four attempts (they happen to be mine) to *say something true* about four different Scripture passages. I offer them not as models of interpretation, but as examples for the many things that can happen in rehearsal, to take us in new and surprising directions. So, for instance, we'll see how a single question can shake us loose from old certainties about a text (Mark 5), to let the characters themselves teach us new ways to speak. We'll take a brave and unflinching look at a very difficult text, a text of terror (2 Samuel 13), to see what could have gone differently if the characters had chosen other verbs. We'll notice how paying close attention to the verb progression in a single verse (Exodus 3:1) can take us "beyond the wilderness" in unexpected ways. And we'll consider how one group's wild (and I mean wild) encounter with the book of Esther led them to ask some of the most serious questions they'd ever asked themselves. Why do we do all this reading of Scripture in the first place? What does it matter, in the end? When there's so much that's evil and false in the world and in ourselves, why even *try* to speak something true? Does reading and rehearsing this ancient text really change anything?

You can probably guess that I believe *it does and it will!*—but I'll leave you to discover that in your own script. For now, pull up a chair, gather a group, and get ready for what's coming. Discovering God's Word in community is one of the best adventures you'll ever have.

❦

I am grateful to Yale Divinity School for the invitation
to deliver the Lyman Beecher Lectures on Preaching in 2012.
Those lectures planted the seeds for this book . . .

. . . which is dedicated to my mother, Anne Babson Carter,
who read every draft, and taught me to live a script with grace.

PART I

Reading and Rehearsing in the Repertory Church

CHAPTER 1

Finding Something True

Reading Alone and Reading Together

Drop-Outs in the Kitchen

If you're hungry to encounter Scripture and meet a living Word, you're in good company. Many of us—people of faith, people with doubts, dedicated churchgoers, and those who are seeking—are hungry these days. We crave nourishment that will sustain us and wisdom that will guide us, and community that will walk with us along the way. We yearn for justice for all God's people and a peace that passes all understanding. We want to meet, to *see* Jesus, as the Greeks said to Philip (John 12:21). And since Scripture is a reliable place to search—in my tradition, *sola scriptura* declares it to be the first and best place—we're eager to read it and follow in the way of gospel.

The problem is that many of us are reading on our own, and that can be slow work. If you're a *solitary reader*, as most of us are, you read by yourself, on your own, and discuss the reading afterwards—in class or meetings or book group or online. And for solitary readers, Scripture can be so dense and so slow that we begin to think we aren't getting anywhere, and wouldn't it be better to leave the reading to the professionals and the speaking to the preachers?

Often, this is exactly what happens. It's not that we think professionals are the only ones qualified to read and speak about Scripture. In fact, our theology tells us just the opposite: the priesthood of all believers opens the task of proclamation to everyone. But solitary readers are at greater risk of dropping out of that priesthood, and a lot of us are in the solitary habit.

The solitary habit can lead to unhealthy patterns. There's plenty of historical precedent for being *community readers,* as we're reminded by Jewish traditions of engaging Torah in multiple voices and conversations, but not many in my tradition know it, let alone embrace it. We have all the elements that could turn our solitary reading around—a great book, the motivation to tackle it, and the theological mandate to do so—but fewer ideas about what to do when we actually get together. For many of us, going solo with Scripture is still the norm, or at least the default position. So is frustration, when we hit a rough spot in our reading.

What we need are more flexible reading strategies to encounter Scripture, so we can lower those drop-out statistics and, together, meet the living Word. Because at the moment, a lot of us are hungry. And a little bored with our reading. And not sure what to do next. We might as well be teenagers at lunchtime who open a well-stocked refrigerator, survey the contents, turn to a parent accusingly, and announce, "There's *nothing* to eat."

Of course there's plenty to eat. What the teenagers are telling you is (1) whatever's in the fridge is in a whole-food state and has to be cooked before it can be eaten; (2) they don't really know what to cook or how to cook it; and (3) rather than learn, they would like you to do it for them. Some parents take on that role and never give it up. But if you want those teenagers to ever leave home and fend for themselves, eventually you have to show them that the pound of hamburger and the green pepper staring at them from the third shelf really can become a lovely spaghetti sauce—if you sauté them with some onion and garlic and olive oil and tomatoes and herbs. Otherwise, you end up with a houseful of entitlement-driven young adults who believe a parent's primary purpose in life is to cook *for* them.

The faith community that lets its people drop out of their calling to read and speak about Scripture will soon be sitting on the best-stocked refrigerator in the universe that no one but the professionals can use. And it won't be locked and hidden away, this incredibly stocked larder that is our Scripture. It will be right there, at the center of everything. In most churches, there's a refrigerator in every pew.

So when the people wander in hungry, open the fridge, and stare at the contents, *surprise*—it won't be clear to them how Leviticus could ever be nourishing, let alone appetizing, let alone dinner. They won't have any idea of where to start, except that it involves a lot of chopping. The refrain will sound: "There's nothing to eat at church. We're hungry; we want some Scripture. Not the Good Samaritan story again; we're tired of that one. Make us something else, something we *like*." And if there's a preacher on hand, and the preacher capitulates, you're off and running with another generation of entitlement-driven folk who are always hungry, always hanging around the fridge, and always thinking that the preacher's primary purpose in life is to wait on them. Why should they know or behave any differently? No one ever taught them how to fend for themselves, to let Scripture be their daily bread. No one ever showed them that church could look like more than the preacher's basement apartment.

You can see what a vicious cycle it can be for all of us, whether we call the church home or have long ago moved out. But the means to addressing it is totally within our capability. As the United Nations keeps reminding us, hunger is the number-one killer on our planet, and not because there isn't enough food for everyone; there is. We simply lack the will to change. We have to learn how to prepare and distribute the food we have—and we must do this with Scripture, too. The survival of the planet depends on it, because hunger of the body and hunger of the spirit will intertwine to devour our species.

Here is what I propose: invite the drop-outs back to the kitchen. Release the wait staff and tie on the aprons. Then open that gorgeously stocked scriptural fridge and, together, learn how to prepare what's in it. Learn to be community readers as well as solitary readers, so we can feed ourselves and others.

As we learn, we can also take a cue from theater studies. Some texts need to be practiced as well as studied. There are times to stop talking *about* Scripture and learn how to live as those who have been set loose with it.

Where the Wild Things Are

The way some church folk talk, you might think Scripture has become as tame and bendable to human will as a very well-trained miniature show dog. But the truth is that Scripture is wilder than anything we can imagine. It doesn't need us to open any restraint gates whatsoever; it is indomitable, intractable, irrepressible, and about as resistant to a leash as any gale force wind. As one of my students remarked in a rather dazed way, after he read Scripture from the pulpit for the very first time, "Whoa—something *happens* when you're up there."

The biblical text is a wild thing, and it takes us to where the wild things are. When we read Scripture in community, we have no idea what will happen or where it will take us, except that whatever it is won't look like anything we know—it is the wild and free vision of God's reign, breaking its way in. It is the mother of all waves carrying us over the known horizon. Maurice Sendak may not have realized he was writing the perfect description of our biblical interpretive task when he wrote his classic children's book, *Where the Wild Things Are*, but he was. Maybe, every time we open our Bibles, we should open our mouths too, with a collective roar: "Let the wild rumpus start!"

For any wild rumpus to begin, however, *we* have to let loose. We need to put on our wolf suits, like young Max in the story, and sail away to where the wild things are. Which is really another way of saying we need a reading space where we can make mischief of one sort or another (as Sendak puts it) . . . with the biblical text.

This could mean a departure from Bible study as we often know it. I once met a man in South Carolina who assured me, "Oh, I could never go to Bible study. I don't know any of the answers." That man was an intelligent, confident, thoughtful person, and he was afraid to go to a Bible study at his progressive church because he feared it would expose his lack of knowledge. Let me add that his congregation had one of the best church educators in the business; it wasn't that she wasn't doing her job. For this man, however, Bible study looked like a school that is teaching to a test: facts, figures, themes, doctrines, and no church person left behind. He believed himself to be biblically illiterate, and for him, this was something shameful, something to hide. His church offered no other way to gather around Scripture, so he slipped through the cracks—and, as a nifty side effect, became totally dependent on his preacher to explain the text to him every week. Which, I'm sorry to say, this preacher really likes doing, and isn't about to give up. Once the cycle of power and dependency starts, it's hard to break.

Maybe it's time for another move entirely. Our Scripture encounters us in so many rich ways. It is a storehouse of knowledge. It is a sourcebook of wisdom. It is also *art*. Poetry, proverb, novella, epistle, epic, memoir, farce, and myth—our Scripture is art in all its witnessing forms. And when you interact with art, you take a different approach. There's a time to talk about it, and then there's a time to be set free with it, to explore where it takes you and the truth it may show you.

When we interact with Scripture as art, we do much better at putting on our wolf suits and making mischief with the text, because we're less self-conscious, less burdened about the outcome. We can switch gears for a while, set aside all the other ways we read the biblical text, and be open to something new.

Here's something else I've learned. When the people of God read Scripture together, in a let-loose, wild rumpus sort of way, with no other purpose than to simply speak and listen to the words that are written, the same thing happens every time: *we discover the script in Scripture*. We see that our biblical text is a collection of scripts that God has given us to rehearse until something true emerges. And we become the repertory church.

The Repertory Church

A repertory company is a small band of actors who perform together regularly. They get to know one another, they build trust, they grow over time, they move into different roles. Because they live in the same area, they put down roots. They grow older together; they are in one another's lives. No one can afford to behave like an out-of-town star, because this is ensemble work. Stars are constantly changing the subject to themselves. Ensemble players don't need to do that. They move in and out of the light and the shadows in big roles and small ones, because what they're most concerned about is finding something true to say together with every script. And they know it requires each one of them to do the hard work of being utterly honest.

When my husband and I lived in Minneapolis, we went regularly to the Guthrie Theater, a professional repertory company, gloriously talented. Every play was worth seeing, and some of them imported big names for the lead roles. But the unexpected pleasure of those years was observing how the same group of actors in the residential company grew over time. They appeared in each play in different roles; we had the fun of watching them pop up, every few months, as entirely new characters—so well camouflaged that you had to pay attention to spot them. No one was ever typecast. An actor who played the king in one production might be the butler in the next, and each role provided a different challenge. The minor roles were often more absorbing to watch—and, I suspect, to play. Through it all, we saw the amazing trust the actors had in one another. It allowed them to take on terribly difficult roles, often in tough performing circumstances—such as presenting three of Shakespeare's history plays, one after another, in a single weekend.

A repertory theater is a powerful witness of what it means to work together on a common vision over the long haul.

Back in college, in that world-opening Theater Studies class—the one that taught me that some texts need to be *practiced* as well as *read*, with others, in community—I had to learn this the hard way. When my classmates and I got our first scene assignment (it was from Shakespeare's *A Midsummer Night's Dream*), we thought we knew what it meant to work together. Actually, what each of us was secretly thinking was, "I know how to do this! Get the plot down and figure out my character's motives. Speak the words clearly and pronounce them correctly. And, most importantly, show the professor I have talent—with a *dazzling* new take on a classic role!"

Off we went in groups of four to do exactly that. And it didn't work. We were rehearsing together, but we were also trying to outdo one another. We had no idea what an ensemble was, no clue that it could be more than mowing one another down with our interpretive brilliance, and no awareness that our star-struck instincts would doom this sort of work from the outset. Our academic training had formed us to be solitary readers in competition rather than a community of readers united in purpose. Only when our professor received what we'd brought to class and then patiently reworked it with us—only then did we realize that what we were dealing with was something so much bigger than one person's talent, or another person's cleverness. The truth wasn't *about* us. It came *through* us. It came through the words of the script that we spoke. But only if our goal was to live in it rather than occupy and conquer it. Only if we had a common vision over the long haul.

In time, our class stopped looking like a roomful of scrabbling, aspiring stars and began working together as a group. We became what our professor was gently guiding us toward: a little repertory company. And then something else happened. We stopped arguing about whose interpretation was the best in all the land. We got over the competitiveness that ran between us, bone-deep. In its place, we noticed some strange new growth. Appreciation. Respect. Trust. Restraint. A generosity of spirit, which flowed into hospitality—even grace.

We saw that the script is so deep that there is always another way to play it, and always another way to read it. And that different casts of players can show you different sides of a scene, and you don't have to decide which one was *right* or *better* or even *definitive*—just which moments were true. And that truth is a current we really do recognize when we're in it. And that it doesn't matter what the source of that current is, whether it came from your performance or someone else's; the joy and momentum you feel is the same. And that any scene can stay fresh, over and over, as long as you're aiming for truth rather than innovation. And that some scenes may not be ours to play right now, but will be later, when life has its way with us. And that there is beauty in the waiting. And that although the script is a given and you can't change the words, you can always change the way you play it—which in turn can change everything.

A repertory company engenders this kind of learning. It isn't a perfect body, nor can it ever be, as my little Theater Studies class so plainly illustrates. Yet even our imperfect band of players experienced moments of truth—more moments than we had any right or reason to expect. Scenes would unfold, and with them, a glimpse of the Beloved Community. The plays of August Wilson and Anton Chekhov, Arthur Miller and Caryl Churchill contained beautiful and terrible visions of our humanity. We saw the worlds we settle for, and the worlds that might be, and how we could choose a life that mattered so that others mattered. We saw truth shining through those scripts and our efforts to live in them. If such revelation is possible in a ragtag body like that, then I wonder what might be possible in a repertory church.

The Word needs a body. It wants to speak through more than one person and interpreter. It wants to speak through every member of the body, because that is the purpose of all our reading and interpreting: to speak of God. To tell what we've seen and what we believe about what God is doing, right now, to liberate creation and set captives free. To be fully awake and alive in the script. That is what a priesthood of all readers and believers looks like when we read together—and we can. When the body of Christ is a repertory church, versed in the script that is Scripture, we become community readers for the sake of the world.

Rehearsing the Script

The best metaphor I know for a wide-open, let's-change-gears sort of reading is *rehearsal*. When we read Scripture as a community, we're doing the same thing that musicians do at band practice, or singers do at choir practice, or actors do in rehearsal: going through the script and practicing ways to play it. Reading the score and learning the notes. Running the lines and building a character. Setting a rhythm and layering beats. Rehearsal is a place to experiment, to try out many possible interpretations of a text. Then we can decide how we want to perform it.

The biblical text offers us more scripts than we could ever rehearse in one lifetime. Every text comes with an invitation to read it—and then *play* it. And the great thing about rehearsal is you don't need much to do it. It's free and simple and easily adaptable to any context. There are really only three moves.

The first is **to gather and let loose**. You need a time and place to read and interpret the script. Not alone. Not one person absorbed in his solitary reading or another in a coffee shop, alone with her laptop. A community of readers, actual bodies, together in a room: *a repertory church*. And then (here comes the fun part) you let loose: set sail for the island where the wild things are, to make mischief with the biblical text. You may have to distribute wolf suits if the level of interpretive dependency in the group is especially high—if, for example, the people don't know that they have the right or responsibility to encounter Scripture as art. It helps if the body knows that the purpose of the gathering is not to make a sermon; good reasons exist for why we rarely throw "Let's Make a Sermon" parties. The purpose of *this* gathering is more exploratory: to rehearse possibilities and enjoy doing it. To set a tone that embraces the free spirit of the venture, while still lifting up the *come back when you find something true* component. As in, you aren't planning to stay on that wild island forever. You're looking to come back with a word of truth—a Word from the Lord. But only after you've had a good rumpus.

The next move is **to read and rehearse**—to actually do it. This is the heart of the enterprise, and also the place where things fall apart if there's no clear direction. It doesn't really work, for example, for the group to gather, read the text through once, and, on a signal, begin to spontaneously howl and dance around the room (while one of you calls to the others, "Go, my dears! Let the text pour forth from you!"). That's just asking for a train wreck. Maybe there are a few very evolved, improvisation-savvy groups out there that would enjoy it, but the rest of us need a little more help. To that end,

I've been experimenting with some ways to get us into the deep end of a text quickly and efficiently, without much ado or preamble. One zooms in for a close and careful reading: "reading the verbs." The other zooms out for a broader imaginative view: "rehearsing the text." For me, reading the verbs (focusing on the action words first) is the backbone of interpretation in the repertory church, and rehearsing the text (using techniques drawn from actors and the world of theater) deepens our connection with it—while bringing out the wild thing in everybody, which most of us need. (Chapters 3 and 4 will teach you the basics of this; Chapter 5 will make sure everyone gets a chance to play. With those chapters under your belt, a good rumpus will be had by all.)

The last move is **to come back and say something true**—to speak about the script in the Scripture that each of you has seen. This is when you sift through the possibilities that have emerged in your reading and rehearsing, and tell one another what you've encountered. You've seen something, so now you say something. About God. For a community, this takes practice. (Chapter 6 will help.) It takes courage and trust and restraint and a generosity of spirit. It takes a repertory church, growing in its appreciation of the multitude of ways God is revealed—in our readings, and in those of others.

I don't know if my professor from those college days would be shocked or delighted to hear it, but all these years later, every time I gather with the repertory church to read Scripture—since that is the script I read, now, and the company with whom I rehearse it—I can picture him sitting in a chair in our circle, and hear his voice as we open our Bibles:

So now let's stop talking about the text.
Let's set you loose with it.
Go rehearse it together, and come back when you've found something true.
Come back and show us, and we'll see.
We'll talk about it, and rework it, and wait for the script that is ours to play.
And then, it's up to you—to live in it.
It's up to you to live a life that matters, for a world in which every life matters.

CHAPTER 2

Setting the Stage

Getting in Motion and Reading the Verbs

One day I was reading a biblical text, playing around with the grammatical parts of speech—nouns, verbs, and adjectives—hoping they might lead me to a sermon. They didn't, and honestly, I wasn't expecting them to. But as I looked at the way each sentence was built, I noticed something that brought my procrastination to a halt.

If you take a biblical text and count all the nouns, verbs, and adjectives in the passage, you'll find a basic ratio: the number of nouns and verbs will be roughly equivalent, and the number of adjectives will be a small fraction—say, a tenth—of that.

What the ratio tells us is that Scripture is good writing. Nouns and verbs predominate, and adjectives are used only sparingly, which is exactly what your high school teachers told you when you were learning how to write an essay in clear expository prose: the best language is language that *moves.* The poet Mary Oliver sums it up for her students like this: adjectives in our writing are worth five cents; verbs are worth fifty cents. It's another way of saying that language is valuable; how we spend it carries weight. And language has to *go* somewhere, not sit around idling and preening its descriptive feathers.

The language of Scripture moves. It is concerned with concrete actions. It prefers to ask "What then shall we do?" rather than "So how do you feel about it?" This is an important clue for us, as readers, because the language of the biblical text shapes the script—and so us, in turn. The language moves, and it invites us to move with it, to trace how the mighty acts of God flow through the text and straight into our lives. As I thought about the parts of speech that day, I wondered how my reading of Scripture might shift if I let the dynamic nature of the language itself—all that movement—lead me. Maybe Scripture was actually calling us to read the verbs first.

Reading the Nouns

Reading Scripture verbs-first might seem like an obvious approach, but it isn't. Most of us enter Scripture nouns-first. And when we do, our conversation tends to get sidetracked. The nouns in the biblical text are just so distractingly *not* of our world. Here are cubits and shekels, arks and archangels, manna and mandrakes, pharaohs and fleshpots. Here are cherubim and Nephilim, Pharisees and Philistines, Samaritans, Syrophoenicians, and divided tongues of fire. The book of Revelation features a seven-horned, seven-eyed, blood-soaked lamb, which should under no circumstances mix with the other lambs and sheep and cows in the Christmas pageant. We don't meet many of these biblical nouns in our neighborhoods today, so every time we turn around, we have to explain one of them. It's a constant reminder that we're reading about a galaxy far, far away. And that, in turn, lets us keep our distance.

The distance hobbles us in at least three ways. The first is that when we enter Scripture nouns-first, we spend a lot of time

translating. The job before us appears to be one of transport: how to airlift all those strange biblical nouns to our own contexts and then connect the dots to a doctrine—a feat which often requires some fast talking and complicated rigging. Meanwhile, we're zipping back and forth between worlds, like little time travelers. The text stays in its own orbit, out there in its own galaxy; we get to live in the "real world," at a safe distance. And the nouns we do unload and unpack look fine in a museum, but they never quite fit in our living rooms.

When we read Scripture nouns-first, we also spend a lot of time **arguing**. That transport move from one context to another, the one that keeps the text at arm's length, allows us to put our own particular brand of literalism on what we read. Curiously, no one is exempt from this; it's a literalism that adjusts to fit any theology, guaranteed. And everyone does it, and everyone picks and chooses when to do it, and it happens all over the church. Here's a liberal version: "Oh, that passage is just referring to a time when women had to cover their heads and keep silent in worship; it doesn't mean that we have to do that today!" Here's a conservative version: "Well, it says right there in 1 Timothy, 'I do not permit a woman to teach a man.' Are you trying to change what it says in the Holy Book?" And off we go, on another round of arguing. It's inevitable, really. Once we decide the job of reading is about transport, we get to pick which nouns to take home.

A third side-effect of entering Scripture nouns-first is that we spend a lot of time **dissociating**. We distance ourselves from certain plots, which of course are set up by the nouns. Here's an example: "The story about the Rich Ruler in Luke 18? That's about money and possessions, sure. But Jesus is just making a point about getting attached to this worldly stuff; he's not suggesting that *every-*

one needs to sell everything they have and give the money to the poor. It's a story for *really* rich people, not us." *If we begin with the noun-driven plot, we get to make that distancing move, which makes us the subject rather than the text.* It allows us to decide which stories are about us and our people, and which aren't; which plots transfer well to our context and which don't; which themes we really need to read and talk about right now, and which can wait—or wait for someone else to deal with. We're chopping the text up, right and left, hacking off the choice pieces we like, and leaving out the bits we don't like. It's an engagement in textual violence we never intended.

Being nouns ourselves, perhaps we can't help it—this compulsion to create distance, pick fights, and dissociate from other nouns that don't look like us—which perhaps a biological anthropologist or a xenophobia expert could explain. But reading Scripture nouns-first really does result in some strange behavior. If you've ever had to listen to a sermon on Mark 2:1-12 that spent fifteen minutes describing housing practices in ancient Israel instead of plunging straight into the verbs that sprint through this story (*paralyze, forgive, stand up, take-your-mat, go, walk, amaze, glorify*), you know what I mean. Nouns are the parts of speech that allow us to isolate ourselves, draw boundaries, designate an "other," and even avert our eyes, as if we didn't want to look at what happens next.

Reading the Verbs

Verbs are different. We all have verbs—the same ones, actually. You and I share verbs with Adam and Eve and Abraham and Sarah and Moses and Miriam and Ruth and Naomi. We share verbs with

Mary and Joseph and Peter and James and John and Martha and Lydia and Paul. We even share verbs with Jesus. That does appear to be the whole point of the Incarnation, doesn't it?—that God came to share our verbs. The Word became one of us and lived among us. Apparently, even God thought the best way to reach us was to meet us, verb for verb. Meet us and raise us and change the whole game.

Verbs are cross-cultural. They can accommodate as many subjects and drive as many objects as you want. They require very little translation work and permit no distance whatsoever. You may not know what a Samaritan is, but you definitely know his verbs (*came near, saw, was moved with pity, poured oil, bandaged, put on his own animal, brought, took care of, took out two denarii, gave, came back, repaid, showed mercy*), and when Jesus tells you to "Go and do likewise," you know exactly what he means (Luke 10:25-37). You also know it's the man's verbs that earn him the adjective "good," as in "the Good Samaritan." If you spend a lot of time obsessing over the geographic noun where he comes from (Samaria), you miss the parable completely.

Verbs also permit very little dissociation. They open up a space that can be occupied by multiple subjects—ourselves included. You and I may not want to have much in common with Cain or Caiaphas or Judas or Jezebel, but they have verbs we know, verbs we have chosen for ourselves. We may wish we hadn't, but we have. Likewise, Jesus in his ministry is constantly turning the tables on us about certain nouns (sinners, tax collectors, scribes, Pharisees) and the verbs we expect they will take. Most often, it is the sinner who *falls down, confesses, loves,* and *thanks*, rather than the righteous person—which scrambles our assumptions about the cast ("us" and "them"), the plot, or the ending.

Enter Scripture verbs-first, and immediately, you're out of the transport business. There is no distant galaxy and nothing to translate. In fact, the verbs you meet are as fresh and recognizable as if you had found them in your own backyard. You want to linger over them, to turn them over and over in your hands, and then take them out for a spin. But it's the other way around. The verbs take *us* out—for a spin, a whirl, and a really fast drive. It's hard to keep arguing about what Scripture means when the verbs keep showing us who we are.

If you're looking for a way to make Scripture relevant, start reading the verbs. You'll have more relevance on your hands than you know what to do with; you'll see yourself everywhere, in verbs you've played. It's the fastest way I know to make a script out of Scripture. And once we have the script in front of us, we can rehearse it to find something true.

Reading Genesis 3:7–8

You don't need to read an enormous chunk of Scripture verbs-first to find a script you recognize; you can do it in just two verses, in less time than it takes to check your rearview mirror. And you don't have to open your Bible any further than the first few pages. The third chapter of Genesis—the story of Adam and Eve in the Garden of Eden—has verbs that would be delighted to rehearse with you. They've been practicing their lines (and yours) for years; they have wolf suits in your size. So let's read two verses in that chapter, to see what might happen.

GENESIS 3:7–8

> 7 Then the eyes of both were opened, and they knew that
> they were naked; and they sewed fig leaves together and
> made loincloths for themselves. 8 They heard the sound
> of the LORD God walking in the garden at the time of the
> evening breeze, and the man and his wife hid themselves
> from the presence of the LORD God among the trees of the
> garden.

Those two verses have a lot of verbs: eight, to be exact. *Were opened, knew, were, sewed, made, heard, walking, hid.* At first glance, they don't seem like very exciting verbs. You wouldn't have to fly halfway around the world to some exotic place to find them. You could run down to the corner store any old day, and they'd be right there in the third aisle, between the cereal and the breakfast bars. What's so special about sharing a script with a Cheerios box? What more can you say about verbs like that?

Everything.

– 1 –
were opened

In your past life, your before-I-started-reading-the-verbs life, verb tense meant nothing to you. You could go days without giving it a passing thought. But look out: now you're the sort of person who knows, and even cares, that Adam and Eve's first verb is (wait for it) *passive tense*. It's a new world, grammarphiles.

The passive tense is aptly named; it means you just sat there like a lump while the verb happened to you. And while we can think of circumstances where this kind of inertia might be nice ("I came home last night to find the floors *were swept*, the dishes *were washed*, and the bills *were paid*"), most of us appreciate a little more involvement when it comes to choosing and enacting our own verbs. I would rather *open* my own mouth, files, options, and front door, for example, than discover they *were opened*. If my day has to start early, I would rather my eyes *were opened* by an alarm clock that I programmed to buzz at six, rather than a bout of insomnia that began three hours earlier.

But there are deeper matters to consider. When I can *open* my own eyes, I control my field of perceptivity. I have the option to see what I want to see—maybe exactly what I want to see. And that may not be enough.

Adam and Eve's eyes *were opened*, and that tells us that an active verb, for them, wasn't enough. They needed a passive verb intervention in order to see what they needed to see. So something else took over, literally making them look—perhaps by reaching across and prying their eyelids open. Now if you think this is easy to do, try it on a friend; it isn't. To grab someone's cheeks, turn her head, and physically point her in the direction you want her to face (while she simultaneously wriggles out of your grasp and squints her eyes shut) is like trying to wrestle a toddler into a snowsuit. Adam and Eve's eyes *were opened*, and that's an impressive bit of choreography. But then, epiphanies—those flashes of insight—usually are.

It can take a fair amount of maneuvering to make us open our eyes. It can even take a shock to the system. When was the last time your eyes *were opened*? It might have been in a moment of national turmoil and unrest; perhaps your eyes *were opened* to the lived reality of others who are different from you. It might have been in a time of personal crisis; perhaps your eyes *were opened* to hard facts about yourself, or those you love. Whenever it was, wherever it was, it probably came with realizations that were painful to see and impossible to ignore.

Adam and Eve ate the fruit they had been instructed not to eat, and their eyes *were opened*. The passive verb demands an active response: no more gazing into the distance, seeing the world as you wish it to be. Time to see things as they really are. Time for some new verbs.

– 2 –
knew and *were*

Flashes of insight are like flash floods; the knowledge comes suddenly, without warning. One moment you're looking at a clear blue sky, and the next moment, you're standing in water up to your knees, trying to absorb the new landscape. For Adam and Eve, the flash of insight was a startling revelation: they were naked, and always had been. And now they *knew*.

The verb *knew* doesn't leave much room for speculation. They didn't *suppose* or *wonder* or *guess* or *imagine*. They *knew*, then and there, without a shadow of a doubt. The evidence was right before their eyes. And once you know, there's no going back, as I recently learned at a car rental agency, when I tried to exit through the "Returns Only" lane and punctured all my tires. Once you know, you can only move forward. Take what you know and drive on, with courage, because the road of denial won't even get you out of the parking garage.

What Adam and Eve *knew*, quite definitively, was that an adjective they had never noticed before had apparently been theirs all along: *naked*. They *were* naked; they *were*! And not just in the morning, after a shower and before they got dressed; not just on a lark, after a morning dip without bathing suits. They were naked all the time, in public, in front of God and everybody (or all the animals, at least), and it wasn't a joke or a fairy tale or a slapstick scene in which the hero's clothes are stolen off the dock. It was a deep loss, actually; an appalling truth. They had thought they were covered, and they were not. They had thought they were protected, and they were not. They were naked: laid bare, stripped down, exposed and vulnerable. And how devastating, not to mention humiliating, to have your eyes opened to the fact that everyone can see you, and even see *through* you—that you've been living for years in front of a window with no shades.

This moment in Genesis 3—when Adam and Eve *knew* that they *were* naked—has inspired more works of art than any other scene in Scripture, except for the Crucifixion and the Nativity. Many of the works depicting the two in Eden show a quaintly innocent couple, modest and graceful, holding fig leaves in the appropriate places; their newly discovered adjective appears to be causing them only vague embarrassment. But there may be more to the picture. These two *knew* that they were naked, and it was a sucker punch of a revelation. The fresco of Michelangelo's Sistine Chapel captures the moment, but so does Edvard Munch's *The Scream*.

– 3 –
sewed and *made*

What do you do when your eyes are opened and you know that you are naked? Crisis management. You get to work on the cover-up. You stitch up a story that you pray will hold. And as this one illustrates, you hope there's more at hand to stitch with than fig leaves.

Cover-ups take some effort. This is as true literally as it is figuratively, which my students and I learned on the day I brought needles, thread, and a big basket of fig leaves from my yard to class, so that we could read and reenact the text: "Adam and Eve *sewed* fig leaves together and *made* loincloths for themselves." Our experiment showed us a few things. If you're serious about concealment, it takes about an hour to sew a loincloth—and longer if you've never held a needle before. Design matters. So do the materials, and leaves aren't a good choice for vulnerable areas. For one thing, they wilt in very short order. For another, they itch. By the time you've finished sewing, you have a limp and ineffectual little green garment that will fall apart at the first good tug—in short, no cover-up at all. If you're going to go to all that trouble, we said to ourselves in disgust, surveying the sad results of an afternoon's labor, you'd do better with animal hide—something durable that might actually last longer than a few minutes. But sewing fig leaves together? That's just a waste of time and energy, and a ridiculous idea in the first place.

Sometimes it takes a literal reenactment of the verbs to show you what's really going on. In this text, it's the fig leaves that get most of the attention, as nouns often do. They're glossy and showy and provocatively placed, and so well known that they've become their own figure of speech. But the text gives us a verb to go with "fig leaves," and that takes the image in a completely different direction. Now, they're more than a cover-up. They're evidence of the futility and absurdity of the whole concealment enterprise: *sewing fig leaves together* so you can *make loincloths?!* That's about as pointless as teaching ants to turn cartwheels, and every bit as ludicrous. Yet it shows us how far human beings will go to cover up their fear and shame, how they'll attempt ridiculously impossible things, like *sewing fig leaves together.* The image is supposed to make you burst into laughter, and then, on second look, tears.

They sewed fig leaves together. What a comic, cosmic mismatch of verb and noun. You can sew hides, but not leaves. You can make wreaths of those leaves, but not loincloths. At the heart of this story is the freedom God gives human beings to figure out which verbs are theirs, and which nouns those verbs can take. *Cover-up* and *mistakes*, for example; *hide from* and *God.* Those are pairings that will never work in the end. But a human being will give it a try.

– 4 –
heard* and *walking

No sooner have Adam and Eve donned their botanical outfits than they realize they have company. They don't need to ask who it is. The footsteps are all too familiar: "They *heard* the sound of the LORD God *walking* in the garden at the time of the evening breeze."

On any other night, it might have been a comforting sound. After all, God isn't *running* or *stomping* or *marching* in heavy boots. God isn't *searching* from house to house, banging on doors. God is simply *walking*, perhaps because it is what God does in the evening: God takes a little stroll, looks at the garden, waters the flowers. On any other night, Adam and Eve might have been glad to hear the sound of those footsteps. They might have poured a few glasses of iced tea and brought some lawn chairs out to the garden so they could all sit down, after their walk, and catch up on the news of the day.

Only it wasn't any other night, and the sound wasn't comforting. When the news you have to share isn't news you want to tell, familiar footsteps and rituals hold no promise of pleasure. They just hammer home what you're going to have to do, eventually, which is to explain your new adjective (naked), your new clothes (fig leaves), and why you were talking to that snake in the first place. The scene that's coming will feature a lot of how-could-you's and why-would-you's about your woeful lack of judgment in consorting with reptiles, and in the end you'll wish you had never heard the word "fruit." So the footsteps are far from reassuring; to the contrary, they're like getting a smoking howler from Mrs. Weasley. They signal that the explosion is imminent. They give you a few frozen seconds to contemplate it, but no more.

– 5 –
hid

Here is the moment of reckoning. Adam and Eve have a decision to make and only a split second in which to make it: God is on the move, coming their way, and what will they do? Will they step up and tell the truth about all that has happened? Will they describe their part in it, from the first big mistake to the string of verbs that followed? And will they do it before the evidence speaks for itself, which it surely will, as soon as God sees their faces and their fig leaves?

In an ideal world, of course they would. They would step out in faith, confident that their most exposed selves would be met with love. They would know in their bones that faith speaks louder than fear, and in their garden, shame has no place. And telling the truth would be as natural to them as breathing. They would *come out* and *confess*, with real remorse, and then *go forth*, having learned from it.

But this is not an ideal world. Something has broken, or is broken, and so the cover-up continues: "The man and his wife *hid* themselves from the presence of the LORD God among the trees of the garden." Notice that these two aren't bothering with fig leaves anymore; loincloths only cover bits and pieces. Now they want an invisibility cloak. They want to disappear completely into the trees, so that nothing about themselves and their story can be seen at all. If they could, they would melt into the background like chameleons, join a witness protection program, and begin a new life in another garden, miles away. But since those options are physically impossible, they do the next best thing—they attempt the theologically impossible. They hide. They hide from God.

There are a lot of things we could say about hiding, whether it be from God or one another, but perhaps the most important thing to say, the most honest, is that *we all do it*—or try, anyway. Hiding is a reflexive human impulse. We hide what we really think. We hide who we really are. We hide what we've really done, or left undone, and we hide what the world has done to us, out of fear and shame. It isn't easy. There are masks to wear and personas to adopt, with stiff upper lips and brave faces. But in the end those are like fig leaves: they wither and fade, slip and fall. There's nothing left for it but to run for the trees.

Adam and Eve *hid* from God. And one of the most beautiful things about this story is that God doesn't abandon them there. God doesn't leave them in miserable isolation, or search them out and drag them from their hiding place. God *calls* them out. "Where are you?" God asks, in the next verse, giving Adam and Eve a chance to come out from their hiding place. It's almost like watching a game of hide-and-seek with a two-year-old: the parent pretending not to see the little arms and legs sticking out from behind the cabinet, calling out for the sake of the game, and a two-year-old's dignity, "Where are you? Come on, now; where are you hiding?"

Reading the Script

At this juncture I should probably say that if you were looking to keep some distance between yourself and this text, *reading the verbs* is not the way to go. You'd be better off with historical criticism or any of its robust offspring, which will offer you a good read at a cruising altitude of 39,000 feet. You will not be required to admit prior knowledge of any verb. You will not have to rehearse or play any of them. You can simply admire the view and go home.

But if you're looking for more than a fly-over, reading the verbs will keep your feet on the ground. The text will become a script that invites you in. It will have verb sequences you recognize and many you have played, and that makes the script one you already know. At very close range.

At first this may not seem like good news. Genesis 3:7–8 hands us a fearsome sequence of verbs: *were opened, knew, were, sewed, made, heard, walking, hid*. They might as well be dominos; tap one, and the rest follow. We know those verbs. We've lived those verbs. Reading them is like being expelled all over again from some fresh, pure place where trust is never broken and people you love are never hurt, and you can stand before God with a clean heart. Reading this text is painful, and all those distancing moves, like dismissing the story as a primeval myth, do nothing to shield us. A primeval myth is still a script—the best of its kind, actually. "Myth" just means the story is brilliant. "Primeval" means it's had a really long run, since everyone, *everyone*, gets to play it.

The good news is that when we read the script in the Scripture, we have a chance to do more than relive our own verbs. We can change the subject from ourselves to God. Only then are we ready to talk, as a repertory church, about the truth we see in this script.

Only then are we ready to say what we believe about a God who will let us choose our own verbs, and then enact with us this elaborate performance of hide-and-seek with fig leaves, of cowering and crouching in thickets of shame until we can summon the courage to say, "Here I am. I'm here."

CHAPTER 3

Reading the Verbs

Jumping Right in with Ten Conversation Starters

Reading Scripture in the repertory church is a community-building experience like no other. You just need a place for everyone to jump in—which is what this chapter is about. To get the conversation started, I'll offer ten questions a group can ask about the verbs in a biblical text. They don't require any special knowledge or degree to decipher; if you know what a verb is, you can do this. And everyone has something important to contribute. Every one of us has first-hand experience of what human beings do with verbs. Reading the verbs in Scripture allows us to talk about *what we know, first*—before we plunge into the mysteries of all that keeps us wondering.

One thing I particularly like about reading the verbs is that it gives me a way to approach a biblical text I might otherwise skip, avoid, or refuse to touch with a ten-foot pole. Our passage from Genesis 3 is a good example. If you've ever walked into a cathedral, an art museum, a church service in progress, or a conversation that featured the words "Adam and Eve" in any context, you've probably picked up on the fact that this story is *big*. It has launched theologies and ideologies, doctrines and debates that pit science against religion, evolution against creationism, women against men, and human beings against the earth itself. It has featured heavily in what the church has to say about sin. I know people of deep faith who are so angry about what this text has done that they can hardly bear to read it. I once spent a day with a group of clergywomen who admitted they had given up on finding anything redemptive in it; environmentalists have told me the same thing. You'd have to look far and wide to find another text that has exerted as much power as this one.

But here's the thing. There are no "harmful" texts. There are only harmful readings of texts. That's a variation of something Konstantin Stanislavski, the great Russian director, once said: "There are no small parts; there are only small actors." It's a way of emphasizing that what we choose to do with a text says as much about us as it says about the text. And since readings are always *from* and *for*—that is, from a particular context, for a particular purpose—it helps to remember that each new day brings the possibility of a new reading. Even for Genesis 3. And especially when we wipe our own slates clean, and begin with the verbs.

The passage is printed here and the ten questions about the verbs follow it. For more nitty-gritty details about process (group structure, sample responses, and the verb-to-noun-to-adjective ratio), see Appendices 1–3.

GENESIS 3:1–10

1 Now the serpent was more crafty than any other wild animal that the LORD God had made. He said to the woman,
"Did God say, 'You shall not eat from any tree in the garden'?" 2 The woman said to the serpent, "We may eat of the

> fruit of the trees in the garden; 3 but God said, 'You shall not eat of the fruit of the tree that is in the middle of the garden, nor shall you touch it, or you shall die.'" 4 But the serpent said to the woman, "You will not die; 5 for God knows that when you eat of it your eyes will be opened, and you will be like God, knowing good and evil." 6 So when the woman saw that the tree was good for food, and that it was a delight to the eyes, and that the tree was to be desired to make one wise, she took of its fruit and ate; and she also gave some to her husband, who was with her, and he ate. 7 Then the eyes of both were opened, and they knew that they were naked; and they sewed fig leaves together and made loincloths for themselves. 8 They heard the sound of the LORD God walking in the garden at the time of the evening breeze, and the man and his wife hid themselves from the presence of the LORD God among the trees of the garden. 9 But the LORD God called to the man, and said to him, "Where are you?" 10 He said, "I heard the sound of you in the garden, and I was afraid, because I was naked; and I hid myself."

– 1 –
Who gets what verbs?

This question is the group version of "So, what did you do today?" You've probably been answering some version of it your whole life—after school, after work, over dinner dishes, on the phone with a friend—and here, you get to ask it of every character who makes an appearance in the story. It's a bit like playing detective in a locked-room mystery: you make a list of the witnesses who were there, invite them to have a seat in the parlor with Miss Scarlet and Colonel

Mustard, and ask them to account for their movements over the last twenty-four hours while the sergeant takes notes. Eventually, even the most verb-entangled case begins to comb out into separate strands. You see the forest *and* the trees, and then the leaves on those trees. And then the ones who are hiding.

For a story that's generated so much discussion and commotion over the years, the verbs aren't nearly as thrilling as one might expect. *Was* and *said*. (The serpent.) *Said*, *saw*, *took*, *ate*, and *gave*. (The woman.) *Ate*. (The man.) They sound like verbs that belong to a domestic scene featuring a kitchen table and takeout pizza—not the kind that could bring down paradise. True, there's a fair amount of disagreement among the characters about what God actually did and did not say about what they shall and shall not do concerning the fruit of this or that tree, and whether they will or will not die if they eat of it—but that only proves that human beings have been arguing about points of interpretation since they rose from the mud and the rib. The debate is not about what to do, but about what the human beings believe *God said* to do. And since God is a behind-the-scenes character until the second half, we have only their recollection of God's commands to go on, and the subterfuge of a serpent to cloud it.

When you make a list of who gets what verbs in this story, you notice immediately that the human beings are doing all of the movement. They *see*, *take*, *eat*, and *give*, and they *sew*, *make*, *hear*, and *hide*. They have most of the verbs, while the serpent—who sets all the action in motion—has only one. The serpent *says*. It chooses to speak, rather than to strike or bite or show its fangs. It knows the craftiest way to infiltrate Eden is to ask a poisonous question: "Did God say you can't eat *any* of this lovely fruit?" So, instead of bothering with invasion strategies that require strings of verbs and armaments, the serpent simply dishes out false information and sits back to watch. It subverts the truth with a lie. Worse, it claims the lie originates with God. It is the original dispenser of Fake News—and all because it knows the power of words. The serpent has been paying attention: words create a world. And words can destroy it.

We've already seen that nouns can be a big distraction in our Scripture reading. But verbs can, too—if we let ourselves get overwhelmed by a lot of "shall nots" and "will nots" and the fluster of a cover-up. Attending to the particularities of *who gets what verbs* is often the revealer of beautiful and terrible truths. In Genesis 1, God only needed a single verb to create the heavens and the earth: God *said*, and it was so. Two chapters later, that same verb in the mouth of a serpent is all you need to overthrow Eden.

– 2 –
What's the order of those verbs?

Stories unfold in a certain sequence. Verbs do, too. If God had *brought* a flood upon the earth before God told Noah to *build* an ark, we would have a very different story. Likewise, if Noah had *brought* two of every bird and animal and creeping thing into his yard before he had *built* an ark to put them in, I doubt that any of those creatures would have hung around for the months it took him to hammer planks together. The sequence of verbs matters, which is why we tell the story of "Noah's Ark" instead of "Noah's Short-lived Zoo," and why characters in a story need to be mindful about the order of their verbs: what they choose to do first, second, and third. As readers, we can also be mindful of it. And all sorts of meaning-making results when we pay attention to the order in which the characters enact their verbs.

Verb order matters in other ways, too. Sometimes, characters talk about verbs rather than doing them, and cannot agree on a sequence, or their memory of one. They may begin to challenge one another about what he said first and what she said next, and why God intended them to do *a*, *b*, and *c*, in that order, rather than *z*, *y*, and *x*. This is what's at stake in Genesis 3: the order of verbs *as God articulated them* is in dispute. It never was, until the serpent decided to run for office. But now it keeps shifting, depending on who's speaking and listening, and to whom. And it doesn't take much to get the ball rolling.

All the serpent has to do is ask one question that deliberately misrepresents God's intentions: "Did God say you can't eat *anything* in this garden?" It's a pouty question, gleaming with malice, and you can just see the subtext that reptile means to leave behind like a shed skin ("What a mean old God!"). The woman corrects the serpent: "No, God didn't say that; God said this." She can quote God's spoken verb order exactly. She can also apply it to the correct nouns; the only forbidden fruit is from the tree in the *middle* of the garden. Clearly, she knows God's rules (you eat, you die), but the serpent contradicts them by calling into question the verbs that will result (you eat, you will *not* die—you will be like God and you will know!). Even the tree seems to collude in the deception with its own tantalizing set of verbs about the amazing benefits of its fruit for the consumer. And before you know it, whatever God said, in whatever order God said it, is completely drowned out by some very loud and persistent flora and fauna. It goes without saying that the verb sequence that follows (*were opened*, *knew*, *were*, *sewed*, *made*, *heard*, *walking*, *hid*) isn't at all the one the serpent guaranteed; far from it. But by that time, the man and the woman are reduced to threading needles for their fig leaves.

Verb order matters. It matters which we choose to enact, and which we remember, and whose version we believe to be accurate and trustworthy. It even matters which version of a verb order we are promised—and on which we decide to set our hopes. Would you rather build that ark now, or wait for the weather to change? Your call.

– 3 –
What do the verb tense and mood tell you?

Verb tense lets you get at the "When exactly did this happen and how long has it been going on?" questions. "You learn whether the character *has done* her homework, *did* it before dinner like she was supposed to, *is doing* it still, or *will do* it, as soon as she stops texting her friends. This gives you the opportunity to exercise your options in various verbal moods and tenses: "Put down your phone and *do* your homework!" (the imperative); "*If* you do your homework, *then* you can text your friends" (the conditional); "*When* you text your friends without *having done* your homework, you forfeit your phone for the evening" (the parental reprisal, second-person emphatic).

Verb tense and mood offer important information. In Genesis 3, for example, there are three imperatives, which tell you God is not negotiating those verbs (*shall not eat* and *shall not touch*), not now or ever. An imperative is a verb you don't have any choice about taking; it's simply blasted to your side of the court, like a Serena Williams first serve at 128.6 miles per hour. On the other hand, Genesis 3 also includes a slippery "when" clause: "*When* you eat this fruit, you *will be* like God!" It implies that the eating is inevitable, forbidden or not—as if the serpent could see the future that's coming, while God remains stuck in some naïve and bygone past.

It's also the quintessential con: "Give us your credit card number, buy this product, and happiness is yours for the taking; you can have it all!" Verb tense and mood exert pressure on the characters to accept or reject certain verbs, with consequences that are real or fabricated.

Verb tense and mood also create distance, or a lack of it. When God calls to the man, "Where are you?," God isn't asking for a list of all the places the man has been that day (". . . the store, the gas station, the drycleaner, and—oh, yes—that tree in the middle of the garden . . ."). God is asking where the man is right now. God wants the man to name it, own it, and stand up and tell the truth about his life in this present moment. The question, and the tense in which it is asked, call for absolute honesty here and now, not partial confessions down the line when the man has had time to consult a lawyer and consider his options. And the man, recognizing this, steps up. He comes out from his hiding place and tells what he has done and why ("I heard you, and I was afraid, because I was naked, so I hid"). Or half of it, anyway ("And I forgot to mention that I ate, and sewed a few leaves into cover-ups that didn't work so well"). Confession takes some practice, even when those past-tense verbs we most regret are behind us.

– 4 –

What do the verbs stir or evoke in you? What do you remember about them from the times you or others have played them?

This question allows you to sift through your own responses to these verbs. Perhaps it's one you've played yourself, many times—this morning at a red light, for instance (when it was definitely called for). Or maybe it's a verb you generally sidestep, or have never had the courage to try. Or maybe it awakens a joyful or painful memory of a scene you've lived or observed. Or maybe it reminds you of your brother, your best friend, your ex, or your dog.

Whatever a verb stirs or evokes in you is fair game for reflection and, if you choose, discussion. In a group setting you don't have to disclose anything that feels too personal, but you might still notice how the verb has left a trail of bread crumbs for you to follow through the woods. More often than not, the trail leads back home.

One memory that stirs for me is sparked by the *shall* and *shall not eat* verb sequence. When I hear those words, I'm suddenly a child again, in the big wide world of all that's possible to cram into my mouth, and the adults around me are doing their best to keep me healthy, hardy, and reasonably well-mannered. The sheer number of *shall not eat* items boggles the preschool mind: eggshells and cherry pits, gum wrappers and Popsicle sticks. Cookies before dinner and apple juice in bed. Candy from strangers and raisins on the floor. Anything at all that was left in the trash. In my house, I learned that if you guzzled milk straight from the carton or licked butter off a knife, the grown-ups frowned, and if you tried to sample a mushroom in the woods, they went ballistic. Eventually the "shall not eat!" list became more or less ingrained, and I knew what was clean enough, cooked enough, and cut into small enough pieces to safely and politely eat. I was judged ready to handle a kindergarten lunch period, a dinner out, and—years later—a party for teenagers where I might or might not encounter adult beverages.

Now that I'm older, or even old, I understand a little more about what those anxious *shall* and *shall not eat* admonitions were about. My grown-ups wanted me to survive and thrive, yes—but they also hoped I would be able to avoid, resist, and abstain when necessary.

Because they knew: sooner or later, the serpent comes along, with its very crafty ways. And oh, what a master of spin it is! "Of course you can eat that! Don't you know how good it is? Don't you know how high it takes you? Don't you want to feel/touch/taste/smell/see/hear the sweetness of the forbidden, *to know good and evil*, like God does?"

And how convincing it sounds! And how repressive God now seems. And how easy the rationalizations. And how mounting the excuses. And how swift the falling back to earth when the flight ends, and the wings melt, and the ropes tighten, and at your doorstep, the heartbreak and misery are waiting to move in.

When I follow the trail of breadcrumbs left by the *shall* and *shall not eat* verbs, I find a script from childhood. I dust it off and smooth it out and remember what it was like, when life in the garden was as straightforward as bread and milk.

And then I wonder if this script might be the one behind our desperate human search for clarification about *what God really said*. Maybe one reason the church fights so much about points of interpretation is that we're terrified of what might happen if we get the *shall not* list wrong, and mistake the serpent's venom for the children's milk.

– 5 –

Are these verbs associated with certain groups or people? Are they used to stereotype or make broad generalizations?

We might as well be open about this. Verbs can be used to stereotype. Sometimes this is vicious, and sometimes it's just ignorant, but it's never benign. The minute you read in the news (as I recently did) that women are less effective on corporate boards of directors because they *talk* a lot, you know you're in the presence of a verb that's doing its darnedest to stereotype.

Verbs can also be used to make broad generalizations. Sometimes this is unconscious, and sometimes it's just plain lazy, but it's hardly ever fair—or accurate. Could we compare the woman's verbs and the man's verbs in the first half of our Genesis 3 passage, and then use them to make assumptions about *all* women and *all* men? Yes, we could. (Wrongheaded, inane, asinine assumptions, but we could.) It might lead us to deduce that because the woman *said, saw, took, ate,* and *gave* while the man just *ate*, women expend five times more active verbs than men do. It might prompt us to conclude that *eat* is the primary verb of concern for all men: that their brains are ruled by their stomachs, that they let women do all the food negotiation and preparation, that they eat whatever is put in front of them, and that if they could, they'd sit in that recliner with a tray of nachos and never leave the house. It might even push us to campaign for legislation to limit men's access to food, since, left to their own devices and singular verb, men are helpless in the presence of a carbohydrate and liable to *eat* all the world's resources. And then the church could follow up with doctrine about Original Sin, and how the male appetite—fatally flawed—brought about the Fall of Man.

We could go on, but you get the point. Using a verb to make sweeping generalizations (wrongheaded, inane, asinine generalizations) about an entire group of people can lead to assumptions that are dubious, ludicrous, or quite dangerous. There isn't a stereotype on the planet that wasn't once a "harmless" generalization. So it's important to be alert to what our *associations* with a verb might be doing to others (forcing them into boxes? flattening them into types? stripping them of their humanity?), whether we intend this or not.

And then the really interesting questions emerge. If there *are* generalizations or stereotypes at work, who benefits from reading the passage in this way? Who doesn't? Do we need to challenge any of our assumptions to have a more open and impartial reading?

For example, in our Genesis 3 passage, we could look at how the woman's verbs have become lightning rods in many cultures for all kinds of negative generalizations about women (who talk a lot, are easily fooled, and will quickly lead a man to ruin). Who benefits from reading the text in this way? Do we need to challenge any of our assumptions about that?

We might also notice that the most stereotypically "feminine" verbs in our passage don't belong to the woman; they belong to the *tree*—which is good for food, a delight to the eyes, to be desired to make one wise, and planted on its own pedestal, in the middle of the garden, where everyone can see it and gaze at it. So why might a forbidden tree be described in this way, as voluptuous and seductive and fairly flaunting its fruit? Does it let the human beings off the hook for taking and eating? Can we blame them for ravishing it? And if we do read the text this way, what other assumptions might be perpetuated about who is to blame in moments of temptation, or just plain *wanting*?

Conversation along these lines may or may not pan out in the end, but naming associations helps to clear the air. Particularly when reading Scripture, which has often been the source of some of our worst stereotype-wielding violence.

– 6 –

If you run the verbs through your biblical echo chamber, what do you hear?

This is a question that lets you get at the depth of a verb as it has resounded through the pages of Scripture. The Bible is truly an echo chamber. A word that appears in one story may reappear in another, many chapters or even books later. Asking "Where have I heard this word before?" is a way of listening for echoes of it, and pondering what those echoes might mean. It's like the difference between hearing a song once on the radio and buying the whole album to play at home, over and over. You hear patterns and harmonies you missed the first time. You hear that one song in the context of the musician's larger body of work.

The verb "call" in Genesis 3 is a good example. When you run it through your biblical echo chamber, you realize this is a verb that pops up all over Scripture. God calls Abraham and Moses and Isaiah. God calls prophets and disciples and apostles. Most of the time, God calls them to "Go!" But in our Genesis passage, God doesn't call the man to go; God calls him to come out from his hiding place. God calls with a question: "Where are you?"

So what might this echo mean? Are we supposed to hold together these two ways that God calls human beings? Does one precede the other—that is, before we can ever answer God's call to "Go!", do we have to answer God's call of "Where are you?" Do we have to name where we *are* before we can prepare for where we might *go*? Is Genesis 3 a story to tuck away for later, so that when it's our turn, and God calls *us* to go, we remember that first we must come out from our hiding place?

The echo could simply be a coincidence, a pretty little melody to hum on the fly. Or it could be something more: a chord that reverberates with layers of meaning. It might even make you want to keep listening and investigating further—like the unaccountable urge to acquire *Abbey Road*, *Sergeant Pepper's Lonely Hearts Club Band*, *Revolver*, and *Rubber Soul*, once you've listened to *The Beatles* (The White Album). That's what makes the echo chamber so much fun: you never know where it will take you, or which bells of recognition may start to ring.

Yet an echo can also be puzzling enough to make you stop and scratch your head. *The woman saw that the tree was good* echoes a refrain we keep hearing in Genesis 1, every time God creates a new thing: *God saw that it was good*. The overlap here is a bit unsettling. Obviously, the sun, moon, stars, sky, seas, plants, birds, and animals are good; God saw that, and so can we. But do we have to sing the same song about forbidden fruit? For me, that causes all kinds of dissonance, as if the serpent really *had* turned the world upside down.

And maybe that's the point. Maybe it's possible to be so far gone that you can look at the very worst thing for your body, the most poisonous apple or addictive opioid, and *see that it is good*. Which is the serpent's warped version of the echo. And a sure sign, once we buy into it, of paradise lost.

– 7 –

If God is a character in this verse, how are God's verbs different from the others?

With this question, you get to make some comparisons between God's verbs and everyone else's. Newsflash: they won't be the same. Scripture tells us right up front that God has the lead role in these stories, and the lead always has more to say and do than the other characters. Even when God isn't in the action, God is always the subject. Everyone on stage is still talking about God, pointing to God, and trying to get a grip on why God does what God does.

God's verbs are generally bigger, stronger, and flashier. When God enters a scene, the action usually ramps up, and you'll notice an immediate difference between the kind of verbs God chooses and the ones assigned to the rest of the cast. God's list is impressive. *Create, give, heal,* and *save. Love, send, raise,* and *open. Make a way through* and *lead a way out,* with game-changing special effects. These are often in direct response to human verbs of need and suffering—which you don't need to be told are legion.

Of course, God's verbs can also be very slow in coming, or absent for long periods, or difficult to take or endure. There are even reports in Scripture that God *floods, smites, destroys,* or *abandons* the ones God holds dearest, which is when God's verbs are the most inscrutable. The pattern and the promise, however, is that God's saving and liberating verbs will come. But it may take time. And *wait* is not a verb that comes naturally to humans, no matter how often it is thrust upon us.

God may not be in the scene at the start of our Genesis 3 passage, but God is still in charge and in control; we have all those imperatives—as well as the reminder that God *made* every wild animal—to confirm it. The creatures are quite clear that God has verbs they don't have. And this line in the sand is what the serpent exploits: "It's not as sharp a line as you think it is! Cross over to God's side, and here's a verb that could be yours: *knowing*! You could know good and evil in one long, smooth, ongoing participle!" It may be the continuous nature of the verb that enthralls the woman most. Or the fact that the serpent dangles it so convincingly, so close to her side of the line.

And then, in the second half of the scene, after being well and duly quoted (and slandered), God finally makes an entrance. You might think it would be with a grand, celestial verb left over from that creation week, but it isn't: no trumpets, no fanfare. Instead, God picks a verb that blends in with the garden scenery and the creatures who live there: *walking*. God takes a human verb. The fact that they have just taken one of God's verbs that did not belong to them is dramatic reversal at its finest. They want to be like God. God just wants to be with them.

God's verbs are not our verbs, until they are. And then we have to make sense of that—or learn how to live with it. The limits of human being and doing, and the mysteries of God's being and doing, are evident at every turn in Scripture. Suffice it to say that someday, God will have a lot to explain. Meanwhile, we have the job of figuring out which verbs are appropriately human and appropriately ours, and which we were never meant to have.

– 8 –
Do any of the verbs surprise you? Why? What were you expecting?

Scripture doesn't always unfold the way we'd like or expect it to—big shocker there—so this is your chance to name those places for the record. To produce a son and heir, did you think God might go with a nice young couple in their twenties rather than octogenarians Abraham and Sarah? Did you think forty years of wandering in the wilderness was a bit excessive? Did you expect, after those forty years, that God might let Moses do more than *look* at the Promised Land from a distance—that, at the very least, God would have given Moses a little retirement home in Canaan with a modest pension to thank him for his service as The Great Prophet, Deliverer, and Giver of the Law? Sure you did. Get in line.

The point of this question is not to whine and complain about *the text that is there*, but to locate where it diverges from *the text you were expecting*. To name the verbs that come as a surprise to you will focus the conversation better than a gripe session—which is sometimes merited, but not always productive. So ask yourself *why* the verb startles you, if it does. Did you anticipate another action? Did you assume a different consequence? Did God go left instead of right and totally fake you out? If it's something that startles you, it's important to name it. Then we can read Scripture with greater honesty and openness to what we might find there, because let's face it: Scripture is *always* going to surprise us. When God is involved, that's a given.

We could ask, for instance, why God would choose to *make* a creature that's very crafty—more crafty, in fact, than any other wild creature the Lord God *had made*. Why in the world would you inflict *that* on the world? Why create something that will contradict its creator and then give it the gift of *speech*, for heaven's sake? Why put it in the garden like a loaded gun? Why let it roam around where the man and the woman live, when it will immediately try to use its adjective against them? Couldn't God have seen this coming? Or was creation more of a "learn as you go" thing: make the prototype, and then fix the bugs (or serpents) in the system?

Or is there something else we're supposed to ponder here, about the nature of God and God's world? Did God always intend for us to have verbs of free will? Is "freedom to" better than "freedom from"? Does a good creation include very crafty creatures, whom God also loves?

Sometimes the questions give you headaches, and you can understand why the church and its scholars have been so preoccupied with them over the centuries. One surprising verb can lead to a lifetime of study and writing and debating and rewriting, and work that continues into the next generation.

And sometimes the questions give you new visions of what our world might be. One surprising verb can lead to a heart opened, and a life transformed, and the energy to go forth and do likewise.

– 9 –
Did you spot any adjectives in this verse?

Once the verbs have had their say, you can return to the other parts of speech that usually get more attention. We've already noted that adjectives appear a good deal less in Scripture than nouns and verbs do. The basic ratio for any given passage is that the number of nouns and verbs will be roughly equivalent, and the number of adjectives will be about a tenth of that. You could say that adjectives are the Times Square of the Bible (and any other piece of good writing, for that matter): they have neon lights around them, screens twelve stories high, and they aren't shy about getting our attention.

Our Genesis 3 passage has six adjectives to consider: (more) *crafty*, *wild*, *wise*, *good*, *naked*, and *afraid*. We've covered most of them in the previous questions, but notice how the verbs make those adjectives pop! The serpent is more crafty, yes—but the Lord God *made* it! The woman *saw* that the tree was good—but also that it was *to be desired*! The woman and the man knew that they were naked—but then they went and *hid* themselves! The verbs give the adjectives more color and texture, which makes any discussion about the passage that much livelier.

Adjective sequence can be just as interesting as verb sequence. Does it matter, in the order of adjectives in this passage, that *afraid* follows *naked*? Is fear a result of exposure? The man certainly tells it that way: "I was afraid, because I was naked, so I hid myself." He didn't even know what fear was until he realized how exposed he was! That could prompt us to talk about what vulnerability does to people—how terrifying it can be, and how risky it can feel, and how it can make us want to run and hide, from God and one another. Then we might wonder: what would it take to replace *afraid* with another adjective? And *hid* with another verb?

– 10 –
And what about those nouns?

The nouns have been cropping up at a steady pace, all along, and like the adjectives, we've reviewed most of them by now. But again, notice how the verbs give those nouns super speed and topspin! Would you care, for instance, whether you were in *the garden* or in *the middle of the garden* on any given day? Probably not. Unless it was lunchtime, and you were hungry. In which case you might want to be aware of tree placement, and exactly where in the garden you go apple-picking. My advice? Avoid that middle section.

As you read the verbs, these ten questions are good tools to keep in your group's kit of possibilities. You don't need to ask every question of every verse—in fact, you probably won't—but in time, they become questions *you really want to ask* when the need arises. That's when you know the script in Scripture is coming into focus with clarity and urgency: you recognize the verbs you've played, and you can't wait to dig deeper. Want to keep the group's energy flowing with even more discoveries? Take a look at the next chapter. We'll return to that metaphor of "rehearsal" with ten more things to try as you read the verbs in the repertory church. Buckle up.

CHAPTER 4

Rehearsing a Text

Reading in Wolf Suits with Ten Things to Try

This book hinges on several claims we've already explored in the first few chapters. That rehearsal is a way of encountering Scripture, for instance. And that reading the verbs is the heart of rehearsal. And that reading the verbs makes a script out of Scripture, so the repertory church—awake and alive in the script—can *say something true* about the living Word.

There have also been a few references to letting loose with the biblical text in appropriate costume wear. A wild rumpus in wolf suits, for example, is completely acceptable.

So let's zoom in on that word "rehearsal" for a moment. Up to now we've been concentrating on reading the verbs where the wild things are, with great gusto and precision: verbs we know, scripts we've played, close encounters of the primeval kind. But a repertory church always has more encountering to do in our quest to find and live something true. Where to turn next? To actors—those great embodiers of all our verbs—for more rehearsal ideas. Actors rehearse every day, work with scripts every day. If we aim to find the script in Scripture, *our* script, why not ask actors how they do it in their work? What can a group of actors rehearsing a play teach a group of Scripture readers engaging a text?

Much more than you might have thought—and more than either group might be comfortable admitting! So, fresh from the rooms backstage, here are ten things to try when rehearsing a biblical text. They're variations of standard rehearsal practices that actors in any production, from a high-school musical to a Broadway hit, know very well. There's nothing new or revolutionary about them, as those actors will tell you, but they're new to us in our context as Scripture readers, and so worth exploring. Besides, the reason they remain standard rehearsal practices, season after season, is *because they work*, and continue to generate new growth each and every time. Every rehearsal is a chance to find something true, both for a repertory company and a repertory church.

But, before you climb back into your wolf suit, one comment. This isn't meant to be an intimidating list, nor is it a command performance (or set of stone tablets) of Ten Requirements for Repertory Readers. You and your group don't have to try every single thing here. But you might pick one each time you get together—some are tactics, others are matters to consider—to see how it goes. On the other hand, a really adventuresome group could easily try them all on the same text without getting bored, because these practices are designed to shed light in different ways. You'll also probably discover that they're great fun. Rehearsal can be as entertaining as it is illuminating.

– 1 –
Staying in the scene.

Sometimes I'm asked what a preaching teacher actually does all day. I respond that my job isn't to help students construct sermons—not at first, anyway. My job is to help them walk straight into a biblical text without stopping and then stay there, and let whatever happens to them happen. Help them plant their feet and keep listening.

In my old theater-studies world, we called this "staying in the scene." It means you don't break character and interrupt the action, once it starts, just because you don't like how this person said his line or that person made her entrance, or because you have a question or a better idea, or you want to try your bit again since you know you can do it much, much better.

"Staying in the scene" is a practical necessity. If nobody learned to do it, we could never rehearse. We would also make the unfortunate error, each of us, of believing that there's no ensemble, that there's only *me alone*, the great star in your firmament; *me alone*, around whom all things revolve. At age nineteen, my college classmates and I could really fall for that one. Our teacher had to remind us that when a scene starts, you don't stay in it for the sake of what you can do. You stay in it for the sake of what others can or might do, as the scene unfolds, and how that in turn will shape you. You stay in it so that, together, you can find something true.

This is a lot harder than it looks. Rehearsal reveals more about the script, but it also (inevitably, maddeningly) reveals more about ourselves. Once you know that, you don't always want to hang around to see what the cat dragged in today, because there's always something, some truth you were hoping not to have to look at again. It's like free therapy with a sledgehammer and an X-ray machine.

The same holds true for reading and rehearsing the verbs in Scripture. Scripture is much better at reading us than we are at reading it, and it takes nerve to read and be read. That can be a surprise for those of us who thought the primary body part required for Bible study was the *brain*. In pretty short order, we find out that skin, ears, eyes, stomach, blood, guts, and *feet*—that absolutely refuse to turn and run straight out of the text—are also intimately involved. We read Scripture verbs-first, and on our feet. How beautiful on the mountains are the feet . . . of those who walk straight into a text and wait for a word to say.

This is especially important when the text we're reading is difficult (which will be the case in Chapter 8, "Staying in the Scene: *Reading and Rehearsing 2 Samuel 13*"). To stay in the scene, no matter how awful the story gets, requires the collective nerve of the group. It also requires great compassion and tenderness for one another. We have to believe, and keep repeating, that there's nothing that can separate us from the love of God in Christ Jesus—not even this text, and the word it is giving us to say.

– 2 –
Blocking the action.

Most Bible studies I've been a part of have been sedentary affairs. We pull chairs up around a table or arrange them in a circle, and we sit down to read and talk. No one moves much. No one moves at all, in fact, until it's time to go. The stillness allows us to settle in and concentrate on the task at hand, but it also means we miss out on some other ways to learn.

One of the easiest ways to engage a biblical text is to get out of those chairs, from time to time, and physically recreate the scene.

Step into the roles of the characters. Do the verbs they're doing; make the gestures they're making. Move around the room, as the text dictates. If Jesus is setting out on a journey, have him pack. If a man runs up and kneels before him, have someone do it. If the disciples are standing in the corner murmuring, put them there. If a widow shouts at a judge repeatedly, get someone to yell at someone else for a full two minutes. When we physically recreate the action, we let our bodies do the teaching. And we notice things in the text we wouldn't have seen or heard otherwise. We may even notice a detail that totally changes how we view the story, or that opens it up to us in a new way.

In stage lingo, this is known as "blocking." Blocking is a theater term that refers to the physical placement and movement of actors in a performance. For the audience, it's the visual picture of the scene: where the actors stand, how they move in relation to each other, what they do with their bodies, and how these movements and gestures convey character and tell the story.

Blocking usually happens on the front end of rehearsal. Some directors will block a scene on the first day, before anyone says a line from the script; others will hold off until rehearsals start, so the actors can be part of the decision-making process. Blocking a scene is like solving a puzzle: how do we position the actors, and move them from one spot to the next, so the scene makes sense? What sorts of visual pictures will we make? How will those pictures create meaning for the ones viewing and experiencing the action? And from a technical viewpoint, will the blocking work on this particular set, with lighting and sound and camera angles factored into the equation? Once a scene is blocked and the actors know where they're supposed to be and what actions they're supposed to do, rehearsal can go to the next level. Everyone can enter the script more deeply.

Blocking a scriptural text gives you a visual picture of the scene and a physical experience to reflect on. The verbs come alive. In my rehearsals with various groups, I've invited members to climb trees (Zacchaeus), sweep the floor (the lost coin parable), lower a person through a window (the paralytic in Mark), and dance around a golden calf (Exodus: the Ten Commandments). We've recreated lion's dens (Daniel), royal feasts (Esther), wrestling matches (Jacob), and giant whales (Jonah). One memorable year, we staged a church fight (1 Timothy) over women's leadership in Ephesus, while someone read Paul's letter as a crisis intervention attempt. With a little imagination and abandon, your group can block just about anything, and your reflection will move to a whole new level. And yes, the neighbors will find it odd, but don't worry; you'll get used to it, and so will they. In a few weeks, no one will even blink when your group decides to recreate the storm at sea so Jesus can walk on water (John 6).

– 3 –
Switching roles.

If you're a child, and your grown-ups have anything to do with church, sooner or later someone is going to draft you into the Christmas pageant. It will probably happen multiple times over the years, because Christmas pageants have plenty of parts for every age group. The good news about this is that you'll rarely play the same role twice. Eventually you'll age out of the sheep and cows in the stable, and move up to shepherds or angels or wise men. You might even be Mary or Joseph, one year, if the pageant director thinks you won't be embarrassed by it, and can sit still for that long. Even babies can be in the Christmas pageant in the starring role; they won't remember it, but they'll grow up hearing about it, knowing they had a turn in the spotlighted manger. Adults who have long since graduated from Christmas pageant eligibility will tell you, in an offhand way, that they were baby Jesus in 1954. It's a point of pride.

I don't remember every Christmas pageant I was ever in, but I do remember some. I remember having to stand with the barn animals, in fuzzy pajamas, and wishing I were old enough to be in the junior choir, so I could wear a red robe with a white cassock and sing with the heavenly host. I remember being thrilled the year I was chosen to play the angel Gabriel, who had real lines and got to sit behind the pulpit and make a grand entrance. I remember being startled and secretly pleased, as a thirteen-year-old, the year I was asked to be Mary—until I heard my younger brother was going to be Joseph. As an older teenager, I remember singing with the adult shepherds' chorus the year our Christmas pageant was a production of *Amahl and the Night Visitors*. And as a parent, I remember the year I had to sneak up front to sit in the chancel with my younger son, who was most reluctant to join the other three-year-old angels in their tinsel crowns, singing "Away in a Manger."

Christmas pageants are annual celebrations for the community, showcases for the education program, and a ton of work for the adults in charge—but they're so much more than that. They are the first place, and perhaps the only place, where we'll learn what it's like to switch roles in our sacred story, and so experience its verbs from another point of view. A child who plays a donkey one year, carefully *guiding* Mary to the manger and then *nestling down* in the straw to watch, will have very different verbs than the year she plays an angel in the balcony, *bubbling* with excitement and *shouting* to shepherds about good tidings of great joy. From her perspective in each role, what she hears, what she sees, and what she knows in her body will be different. Next year, maybe she'll be a dove in the rafters. Or a shepherd in a field. Or a wise man from afar. Or an innkeeper with no more room. Eventually, she may play all those roles, each with its own set of verbs. And every one will show her something new about what it means for us that God came into the world as a tiny child to a poor family that was far from home, with nowhere to stay.

If you're in a group that reads Scripture together, you might want to tap into that Christmas pageant mode of being and doing. Switch roles in the text to try out new verbs. And be intentional about it. Begin with the characters that seem most natural to play, and then pick a new role. Audition for another part that goes against type. Try reading from the point of view of the prodigal son, then the older brother, then the father: what do you notice? Try standing with Pharaoh, then Pharaoh's daughter, then Moses: what do you hear? Be a disciple and then a Pharisee, a leper and then a priest, a prophet and then the wayward people, a slave and then a landowner. There are so many parts to play in the text, with so many verbs, and each part is worth playing more than once. Each story is worth its own annual pageant—and carries its own verbs, action, motions, and intentions. Your group might designate a casting director for the day, so to speak, and have them assign roles. And then switch.

– 4 –
Changing the verbs.

One of the things I love about Scripture is that it's a given. It's a script that's already published and printed, so we have to deal with it; we have to play what's there, in the translation before us. We have to step into certain roles we might have written differently, if it were up to us, or play verbs and scenes we would gladly have edited. Sometimes this is easy to do and sometimes it's not, but the challenge to find something true within certain prescribed limits is a spiritual discipline. It means we have to rehearse long and hard, and read deeply, and speak honestly—about what we see, and what we don't see.

Reading the verbs helps us focus on some of the text's givens. What verbs are actually right before us in this verse? What verbs are we going to have to rehearse? Which verbs belong to which characters, and what does that tell us about them? What's the order of those verbs? Does the progression enlighten us? (Chapter 9, "Changing One Verb: *Reading and Rehearsing Exodus 3*," takes a closer look at this question.) If we were to make a list of each character's verbs and compare them, what would we discover?

When I read Scripture, I pay close attention to the givens. But I also grant myself permission to speculate and ask questions. Why is this verb here, as opposed to another one? If this one is surprising, what verb was I expecting to find? If I could change the verb that's given, what verb would I substitute? How would that alter the story? And if we were to continue in that vein, where are the places in the text where everything could have gone differently, if someone had chosen a different verb?

There are two reasons why this is a helpful exercise. One is that it prompts us to name the places in the text that create tension for us, and it helps us to think about why. Are we troubled when the text says God *slew* or Jesus *wept* or Sarah *laughed* or Peter *denied*? Are we shocked to hear Jeremiah *cry out* that God *has deceived* him? What if an angel *announces* or a great fish *swallows* or Paul *heals* in some miraculous way? If the verb bothers us, perhaps it's rubbing up against our theological convictions, or ethical principles, or scientific paradigms, or plain old common sense. Changing this verb—just to speculate, for a moment—can shed light on a tension we might not have noticed otherwise.

Another reason to ask pointed questions about the given verbs in a text and to experiment with changing them is that this exercise helps us to think about the verbs we choose in our own lives, and how our stories might unfold differently if we chose new ones. If Scripture is a script that's already published and printed, our lives—at least in the time that is before us—are not. There are verbs still to choose. There are narratives still in process. Asking how a text might go differently is another way of asking how our lives might go differently. It is an act of imagination, truth-telling, and hope.

– 5 –
Going underground.

Rehearsal is a time to experiment with "What if?" questions. What if we did this scene as if we were housewives in Atlanta, or hipsters in Brooklyn, or teenagers in South Side Chicago, or a retired couple in Miami? What if we did it as if we were farmers, or factory workers, or stockbrokers, or candidates in the next election? What if we played the whole scene as if we were bored, or exhausted, or late, or angry? Or unemployed, or undocumented, or newly diagnosed, or secretly in love?

"What if?" questions can change a reading faster than anything else. They're great fun to try and challenging to do; the actors have to stick to the script while changing just one variable. Directors often toss out "What if?" questions as a way to get imaginations moving in rehearsal—even if it's obvious that the final performance won't have a single hipster, farmer, or stockbroker in it. The aim is to keep exploring and remain open, while continuing to learn about the script.

One particularly effective "What if?" question for Scripture-reading groups is to ask what might happen if we read the text as an underground community of believers. What if we were living in a place and time that was hostile to people of our faith? What if we could be arrested or even killed if our gathering were discovered? What if the way we were interpreting Scripture went against the interpretation of our emperor, our slave master, or our faith leaders? What if those power figures had outlawed our reading, or our literacy, or our possession of the Bible itself, because they feared what we might do with it?

This is a powerful way to read Scripture as a group. For one thing, it's a stark reminder of how those in the text often had to hear and tell it themselves: by hiding their identity and going underground. Scripture is filled with stories of how the people of God endured seasons, even centuries, of terrible oppression and persecution when who they were and how they worshiped were under constant siege. Hebrew slaves in Egypt; Jewish exiles in Persia; early Christians in Rome: each had a Pharaoh or a Nebuchadnezzar or a Caesar to contend with. They had to meet in secret, pray in secret, pass down their sacred stories in secret. It's a sobering experience to read as if we, too, were in the catacombs.

But underground faith communities are hardly limited to the pages of Scripture. They exist now, and have existed in every age—and those painful memories, those shocking stories, are part of our history and part of us. African-American slaves who met secretly in hush harbors; Jews in Nazi Germany who said their prayers in hiding; Christians in communist countries who smuggled Bibles between houses: the stories go on and on. The fact that we can freely gather, out in the open, to read and rehearse Scripture *as our script* is a blessing we might easily take for granted. Doing an intentionally "underground" reading ensures that we won't. It also begins important conversations about who our ancestors were and how they interpreted Scripture. Descendants of slaves and descendants of Pharaoh have deeply buried lenses to ponder, and truths to speak and hear.

– 6 –
Asking new questions.

It probably goes without saying that all this switching around and changing it up will result in new questions. And that's exactly the point. We try new things in rehearsal so we can ask new questions of the text. These lead to new insights and, with time and patience, perhaps to something true. But it's a hard road to get there, and the text isn't known for making it especially easy on anybody.

One way to stimulate new questions is to read with new people (as happens in Chapter 7, "Asking New Questions: *Reading and Rehearsing Mark 5*"). Change the bodies in the room, and you change everything: contexts, life experience, points of view, angles of vision. You also open yourself to new questions, many of which you might never have thought to ask. Perhaps you simply couldn't see to frame them from where you sit, or perhaps they aren't questions that were in your best interest to ask. All sorts of things are possible when the perspectives in the room shift.

You might also want to underscore a mantra of teachers everywhere: There is no such thing as a stupid question. That goes double for groups that are reading Scripture. Too many of us are worried that our questions aren't worthy or faithful or relevant or even appropriate (since this is the *Bible*). Maybe we think we should have picked up the answer years ago, sitting in church. Maybe we think we should have learned it in school. Maybe (and this is the teacher's and preacher's particular bane) we think we're supposed to be the ones who have it all wrapped up, and it would be scandalous to admit otherwise.

You may want to initiate a conversation about what, exactly, constitutes a stupid question by asking each person in the group to describe one. It will probably be a relief to hear that others get worried about this, too. Air those concerns, and then make a pact that there will be no dramatic sighing, gasping, or eye-rolling every time someone asks a new (not stupid) question of this text we're all trying to encounter. Who knows? It may be the very question to point us toward something true.

– 7 –
Pushing the limits.

In rehearsal, actors have to push the limits. A good director will create the space for that: give them the freedom to try new things, go new places, and push right up to the edges of what seems possible, for both them and the text—*within the safety of set-aside rehearsal space*.

Here we need to clarify two things. The first is that pushing the limits in rehearsal is very different from pushing the limits in real life. Rehearsal isn't a time for everyone to tap into their inner toddler or teenage rebel and throw tantrums, just for the fun of it. Rehearsal is a time for the very careful, very deliberate pressing against boundaries we *assume* to be true, in order to learn more about what *is* true. Another way of saying this is that there are limits to what "pushing" looks like. We can't change the play. We can't change the cast. We can't physically hurt or violate one another. But we can suspend judgment about what we think we know in order to find something true we never knew was there.

A second clarification is that pushing the limits in rehearsal only happens in set-aside rehearsal space. It doesn't happen in your living room, your marriage, your workplace, or your friendships. We don't have permission to act up all over the place (although the off-screen behavior of some actors might make you wonder), nor are we invited to wear wolf suits and make mischief of one sort or another—to paraphrase Maurice Sendak again—*all day long*. It would be exhausting, and perhaps unhinging, for some of us, and, as Max learned, it might land us in a very long and decisive time-out. The wild rumpus of rehearsal needs certain controls. You have to set sail for the island where the wild things are, and there, you can roar your terrible roar, and so on, until it's time to stop rehearsing. Then, as Sendak writes, you sail home, into the night of your very own room, where your supper (or Max's, at any rate) is waiting, still hot.

Groups who gather to read Scripture might spend some time reflecting on this. How will we push the limits of what we think we know, and how will we create an appropriate space to do that? Can we tolerate a little dissonance, for example, without shutting down? Can we consider a new question without worrying about heresy? Can we stomach a little foolishness in the pursuit of wisdom? These are important questions to ask. If the answer is "No way," then rehearsal, for this group, probably won't push against much. It won't take anyone anywhere they haven't already been. But if the answer is "Yes" or "Maybe" or "We hope so," then an adventure, or at least a good sail and a rumpus, are quite possibly on the horizon.

– 8 –
Failing gloriously.

Some days, rehearsal just flows. Other days, it doesn't. The reading you just concluded, the one that you thought might actually lead somewhere, turns out to be a dead end. The next one does, too. And the next one. It's not that your group isn't enjoying the process; you are, mostly. It's just that you aren't reaching the inspirational heights you were hoping to attain. Not consistently, anyway. Or not for a while.

On days like that, it helps to remember what actors say about dead ends: they expect them. They prepare for them every day and actually stride right out to meet them, because the dead ends are vital indicators. Dead ends, blind alleys, and brick walls tell us where *not* to look, where we're likely to find only the shadow side of what we seek. And in order to find something true, we have to peer down many paths that are not.

So encourage your group to be of good cheer. Let the *via negativa* teach you as much as the road that leads to truth: mark it as a dead end and move on. No reading ever fails miserably. It fails gloriously, because you had the courage to seek, knock, try–and try again.

– 9 –
Arranging the space.

Rehearsal space matters. That will come as no surprise if you've been reading up to this point. And while you may not have much latitude here—access to a 60,000-seat Olympic stadium, for instance—you don't need much to read and rehearse well.

Ideally, there's a seat for everyone. Perhaps a table for you to sit around. Copies of the text (I like to print them out in large type) and a board or tablet for making charts or lists. Internet access or reference books. A lighted candle, because it's sacred time, and snacks to share, because chocolate helps. And since blocking is so much fun, room to move. You might push the chairs back or clear space in a corner for the times when you need it. You can even go outside, if weather permits. Think about the accessibility needs of your group, and arrange the space to suit. Exploring the biblical text always involves choreography.

– 10 –
Allowing the time.

All of this takes time. There's a reason why theater companies rehearse a play for weeks or even months before they perform it. They need the time to try new things, take big risks, fall down, get up, and try again. Eventually, it will form them into a community of trust. It will cement their relationships as friends and colleagues. And it will make the play better. In the end, it's all about the play.

For those of us who want to read and rehearse Scripture, there are two big lessons to take from this. One is that we need a significant block of time to do the work. It doesn't need to be an iron-clad commitment to meet for six hours, every Wednesday afternoon, *no matter what*; unless you live in an intentional community, or on Gilligan's Island, that may not be practical. But we do need longer than half an hour together, once a month. We need enough time to talk and muse and wonder—to really rehearse. You might contract to meet for an hour every week, or a couple of hours twice a month, and see how it goes. The group can decide what it can reasonably do, and then set a beginning and an ending date, so no one feels trapped for eternity.

Another big lesson is to take the long view. None of this group-building and trust-forming will happen overnight. Rehearsal is a process of discovery, and it requires patience. You have to be willing to ask questions that will lead nowhere, or try things that don't ultimately work. You also have to be willing to come back, after rehearsals like that, in the hope that today might be the day to find a truth that's waiting, just around the bend. Give it time.

Something begins to take shape when we read the verbs and rehearse the text with the questions and ideas from these last two chapters: our body, our community of readers, moves and shifts toward a hovering place of vision. Maybe it's the discernment process taking its natural course. I'm more inclined to say it's the work of the Spirit. I didn't used to speak in that manner—my theater-studies compatriots might find it blasphemous in another sense—but I have experienced the luminous quiet that surrounds a group when the verbs take hold, the script emerges, and the faces around the circle grow still with recognition. We aren't seeing the same script. We don't suddenly agree on everything. But we know we're in the presence of something holy. And it's hard to discount your neighbor's point of view when you can see the light dawning in her eyes.

When that happens, when those scripts in Scripture begin to appear, it's important that the group has a structural base it can trust to hold it. No one wants to say something true that the rest of the group will immediately shoot down. So while we don't (and won't) have the same flashes of insight, big or small, we do need a common code of hospitality to ensure there's plenty of room for everyone to read and rehearse and speak. We need rules of fair play: sandbox rules. And that's what the next chapter is about.

CHAPTER 5

Playing Fair

Digging in Sandboxes with Ten Rules of Etiquette

I would love to be able to tell you that when we get together to read the verbs and rehearse the text, it's always a smooth sail to the island where the wild things are. The sea is calm, the boat is sturdy, and everyone finds a wolf suit (and verbs) in their size. No one tries to dominate or control. There are no skirmishes between alpha males. Rumpus behavior is above reproach. In fact, group dynamics among us are so wondrous that word spreads to the mainland, and reading the verbs in the repertory church becomes a model for world peace.

I live in hope. In the meantime, I live by sandbox rules: ten rules of etiquette for playing fair.

Reading Scripture together can be an exhilarating experience, but also a tender one, so a few protective ground rules are always in order. We know what the biblical text is capable of doing; chances are good that *our eyes will be opened* to various things we may not have been expecting to meet. It helps to know the others around you are committed to being open, gracious, and kind. It also helps to have certain protocols for taking turns and playing fair, so that no one is singled out, left out, or made to feel a stranger. When there is hospitality and respect among readers, rehearsal is a joy.

A group can certainly invent its own set of ground rules for reading Scripture together in the repertory church. But you're also welcome to use these if you'd like to bring some levity to your rumpus.

The Eternal Lightness of Sandboxes

When my children were young, they loved sandboxes, and so did every other child in their orbit. Each of my sons could play well and happily in a sandbox for an hour or more—but only, I noticed, if he was by himself. Add another child to the equation, and it was a different story.

Children seem to find more ways to torture each other in sandboxes than anywhere else. The most tantalizing verbs (*throw, bonk, push, flatten*) find new scope for expression when sand is the medium and shovels are involved, and even the most amiable child is tempted. Let two or more children enter a sandbox, and you need adult supervision. You have to regulate a few things so the children have room to play, explore, and interact safely. You need sandbox rules.

Our family's sandbox rules were pretty ordinary, I thought. "No hitting," for example; that was about as standard as it gets. So was "We don't throw sand at each other" and "We only demolish our own castles, not our neighbor's." I assumed that most families subscribed to a similar set of principles, and that sandbox rules were as generic a code of conduct as one might expect to find in any nursery school playground. I was mistaken.

It wasn't long before my children and I learned that the verbs out there in the sandbox world are fierce, and different families have different sandbox rules. Just because we didn't grab buckets, topple toddlers, or wield shovels didn't mean that everyone else behaved in the same way with their verbs. Some parents didn't seem to mind if their child knocked down another child or stomped on her sandcastle. Others looked on benignly as their children slung sand or poured it down a baby's diaper. On the other end of the spectrum, there were parents who hovered over the heads of their children, issuing a constant stream of directives and critique. It was eye-opening to see how something as innocuous as a sandbox could become a showcase for parenting styles, moods, and verbal tolerance. You can learn a lot about a family from its sandbox rules.

I could always tell fairly quickly whether a family lived by the same rules of fair play we did. If a parent was inattentive or indulgent, or so high-strung that they interfered at every turn, I would know to steer clear. No matter how much I liked them or how much we had in common, a play date with them simply wasn't going to work out. But if a parent was kind and watchful, clear and steady—those were good indicators. Maybe this was someone who shared our sandbox rules. Maybe we could trust one another with what was most precious to us: our children. And, in time, maybe that would lead to friendship.

One of the big lessons of parenthood, and also one of the most surprising, is simply this: you make friends with the families you interact with most. If you can trust your children to one another, then you have common ground, and, as it turns out, the most important common ground there is. Everything else—politics, religion, background, vocation—becomes secondary. You grow more tolerant of one another, more loyal to one another. You listen better and share more, because parenting is hard work, and we need all the help and encouragement we can get.

When my children were young, I spent time and became close with people I might never have connected with otherwise. If we had met at a rally or a debate or a cocktail party, we might have found ourselves on different sides of the room, with different interests and agendas. But we didn't. We met over a sandbox, where we discovered we had the same sandbox rules about the verbs of fair play, and that opened up a world of possibilities. We started to trust one another, and trust is the first step.

Bringing the Sandbox to the Repertory Church Group

Some years ago, I began to wonder what sandbox rules might have to say in other contexts—like a repertory church group. After all, Scripture is one of our most precious things. We want to read it and share it and dig into it together. But we don't always trust it in one another's hands.

We have good reason to be hesitant. History and experience have taught us that (1) we will interpret Scripture differently, (2) difference makes us uncomfortable, and (3) we don't always handle that well. We've been known to inflict terrible violence on one another over differences of interpretation. We've used the worst verbs at our disposal. Sometimes we've even put our most precious things at risk in order to prove a point.

A story in 1 Kings (3:16–28) illustrates this vividly. Two mothers approach King Solomon with a terrible dispute. Both women have recently given birth, but one of the babies has died in the night. Each woman claims that the living baby is hers, and that the dead baby belongs to the other woman. They argue and plead before the king until he silences them with a pronouncement. "Bring me a sword," he says. "We will cut this living baby in two and give half to each mother." Then he carefully watches the women's reactions, which tell him the truth of the matter:

> 26 But the woman whose son was alive said to the king—
> because compassion for her son burned within her—"Please,
> my lord, give her the living boy; certainly do not kill him!"
> The other said, "It shall be neither mine nor yours; divide it."
> 27 Then the king responded: "Give the first woman the living
> boy; do not kill him. She is his mother."

In these days we need the wisdom of King Solomon: *We do not cut our most precious things in half in order to prove a point.* A living child, a living Word, is our main concern. Those lives always takes precedence over interpretational disputes and truth claims. If an argument imperils the life of our children or the life of the Word, then it isn't worth winning.

Maybe it's time to back up a few paces. What if our first question wasn't "Who owns the truth?" but "Can I trust you with *my* truth?" What if we let sandbox rules be the first point of encounter?

Several things might happen. The first is that we might actually be able to gather around Scripture with those who think and believe differently than we do. The second is that our ground rules for reading would enable us to trust one another with what is most precious to us. And the third is that we might have a chance, a real chance, of discovering where that trust might lead. A future we cannot imagine might be open to us simply because we trust that we can walk into it—and the repertory church could help lead the way.

When your repertory church group gathers to read the verbs and rehearse the text, try these sandbox rules. Post them on the wall where everyone can see them. Then you'll be able to refer to them or point to them if you need them–which every group does from time to time. It helps that they're light-hearted enough or even silly enough to break the tension with a laugh ("Oh, dear–I think someone threw a shovel with that remark!"). Sometimes a little humor is exactly what we need to get serious. With a few ground rules, the real work of the sandbox–and the repertory church group–can begin.

Sandbox Rules for Reading Scripture Together

– 1 –
Sand is fun.

Let's start with the obvious. Sandboxes are supposed to be fun. If they weren't, children wouldn't bother; they'd never set foot in one. Of course, sandboxes are also hotbeds of imagination and creativity, not to mention excellent places to bolster a child's social, cognitive, and physical development, but only the adults will tell you that. Children like sandboxes because they're *fun.* The other benefits–and they are truly wondrous, when you think about it–follow. That is by design.

The same holds true for groups reading Scripture in the repertory church: *it's supposed to be fun.* Sweeter than honey, better than gold, and a song wherever we make our home, the Psalmist says; a joy and delight of the heart, in Jeremiah's words (Ps. 119:103,72,54; Jer. 15:16). We read the verbs and rehearse the text primarily because it brings us joy. All the other good and true reasons—to be inspired and instructed and enlightened and saved—follow, as surely as day follows night. They're the adult version of fine and gross motor skills. But they come joyfully; they come when we're engaged in the work that gladdens our hearts. This is a sandbox rule to take seriously. If reading Scripture together creates more anxiety (or fear or anger or boredom) than joy, something's out of sync.

– 2 –
Sand is messy.

You don't send a child to the sandbox in her best dress and expect her to keep it spotless, because sandboxes are messy places. They're gritty and grimy and even muddy at times; there are sticks and bugs and puddles. The child is going to get sand in her hair and shoes and down the neck of her shirt, and while most of this brushes off easily (one of sand's most excellent properties), her clothes are going to look slightly worse for wear. So dress her in old playclothes and turn her loose. Let her make as much of a mess in that sandbox as she wants, and expect to do a lot of laundry. Sand may be messy, but it's nothing a good broom and a sense of humor can't handle.

Reading Scripture is messy, too. Let's just acknowledge that, right off the bat: you can't read Scripture without being changed. Your repertory church group can't read Scripture without being changed. And the change, of course, is good and true and necessary; it is holy work. It's also hard work. Your group will have to rethink, reorder, reimage, and repent. You'll have to wrestle through difficult concepts and stomach impossible stories. You'll have to live with dissonance, or, as we often say in my world, *live in the tension*. That requires a certain tolerance for mess. It helps if you all know this ahead of time, so you don't show up in a "dry-clean only" state of mind. Come ready and dressed to dig. Whatever you wear—that old pair of jeans, that old point of view—is going to get full of sand.

– 3 –
Shovels are for digging, not hitting.

Tools aren't essential in a sandbox. All you really need to build that sandcastle is your own two hands, which can perform any scooping, tunneling, molding, and raking just as well, if not better. But tools bring a measure of excitement to the work, and children like to use them. They also like to experiment with them: a shovel is good for digging—but wait! Would it also be an effective weapon?! The answer is "Yes"—and then it's up to the grown-up to help the child differentiate between appropriate and inappropriate verbs for shovels. *We don't hit with shovels. We dig with them. Otherwise, we forfeit both the shovel and our turn in the sandbox.* Tools are learning opportunities. Give a child a shovel, and you teach him to dig. Give two children shovels, and you teach them to *choose* digging over all the other power-related verbs available to them, none of which have to do with shoveling and all of which have to do with territorial domination.

Groups that read Scripture in the repertory church can definitely use some tools and benefit from doing so. Dictionaries, concordances, encyclopedias, and commentaries from every conceivable school of scholarship help us to dig into the text more deeply. So does theological training, both formal and informal. As long as these tools are used to open and extend the conversation, they can be life-giving for everyone. But when they turn into weapons, it can take down the whole group. No one likes to be hit over the head with everything you know. Aiming a scholarly resource at someone in order to hurt, humiliate, or exclude them is even worse. This sandbox rule is crucial for the well-being of all: shovels are for digging, not taking over. Choose your verbs carefully.

– 4 –

Don't be bossy. Let others build in their own way.

When children build with sand, they explore basic engineering principles: structure, design, form, function, maintenance, support, and problem-solving. It doesn't take long, for example, to learn that buckets hold water but sand does not. On the other hand, wet sand is fine for patting into shapes and molding into forms. It works much better than dry sand, which is mostly good for sifting and sprinkling. The more time children spend in a sandbox, the more they learn, the more elaborate their structures, and the more willing they are to share their knowledge—too willing, sometimes. A five-year-old who has mastered Sandcastles 101 is keen to be the lead engineer for everyone else's projects. You'll need to curb her enthusiasm by reminding her that she isn't the boss of the sandbox; each of us is entitled to build in our own way. A sandbox is a free zone.

One of the gifts of reading Scripture with a repertory church group is the opportunity to hear from each person present. There's always another angle, another view to explore. There's always another context to consider. Some of us may have more experience or expertise with Scripture, but that doesn't make what we see and hear in the text more valuable. So exercise some restraint. Listen more than you speak. Ask more than you answer. This will help your group to guard against self-appointed censors, dogmatists, or spokespersons. It will also allow each of you the freedom of honest reflection, which in turn will engender trust. It's always more interesting, in the end, to ask, "What is it about your life and context that leads you to hear this in the text?" Before we decide what's *permissible*, let's hear what's *possible.*

– 5 –
You can knock over what you build, but not what someone else has built.

One of the best things about sand is how amenable it is to demolition. This is extremely helpful when children are feeling out of sorts and need to pound on something besides their siblings or the furniture: send them to the sandbox, help them slap together a quick sandcastle, and tell them they can smash it all they want. It's quick, satisfying, and can be repeated as many times as necessary. But children do need to understand that we only bulldoze our own structures. Wrecking your brother's castle, just because you think it's better than yours, is unacceptable. So is returning wreck for wreck; we don't escalate the conflict by retaliating, or pretending that a direct hit was an accident. When emotions are high, children may have to work at this rule. A castle in the sand is a tempting and easy target. So is your brother, once you figure out that knocking over his castle can hurt him more than if you knocked *him* down.

I've spent way too much time listening to scholars torpedo one another's work. It's an occupational hazard: academics are supposed to prove the strength of their arguments by pointing out the holes in everyone else's. While this may be appropriate for some venues, it really isn't for a repertory church group. When we gather to read the verbs and rehearse the text, we're not evaluating finished work;

we're gathering ideas. We're holding up interpretive possibilities. We're riffing on themes, like a jazz quintet, and we need the freedom to keep asking "What if . . . ?" So to knock down each other's ideas, out of carelessness or spite, will sap the energy of the group as fast as you can say "sour grapes." Teachers and preachers especially need to remember this. When it seems like everyone else's insights (and sermons) are more brilliant than yours—and who doesn't feel that way, now and then?—resist the impulse to sneer and scoff; it will *not* make you feel better. Go pound on some sand instead.

– 6 –
Be kind to babies and toddlers, who haven't learned the rules yet.

Sandboxes are open to all age groups. This means that sooner or later, some toddler is going to lurch through the play space of older children, crashing into their sandcastles and razing the patient work of the last thirty minutes. It isn't fair (as the child will tell you, in tears), and it isn't right (as the child will bellow into the face of the toddler, causing more tears), but it happens. It's also an opportunity to teach the older children to practice patience. Babies and toddlers don't know the rules yet; they can't be expected to behave better. But we can ask their big sisters and brothers to be patient and kind and help them learn.

Reading Scripture with a group in the repertory church is open to all ages too; more significantly, it is open to all levels of experience. This means that sooner or later, persons who have never opened a Bible may sit down with persons who have been reading it all their lives. They will surely learn and benefit from one another's perspectives; that's a given. But if the more experienced ones find themselves impatient with those who are new to the practice, then we have a sandbox opportunity. Be kind. Be patient. Practice hospitality. This is how we help one another to grow in the faith, and everyone—*everyone*—has more to learn. Besides, each of us is a toddler about something, when you think about it. Each of us is staggering through some realm of experience (bumping into things all the while) that others know much more about than we do. We can all use a little hospitality from the big kids.

– 7 –
If you need help, ask a grown-up.

Even when everyone is doing their best to follow the rules, things don't always go smoothly in a sandbox. There may be one child who flat-out refuses to share, or another who is deliberately hurtful. There may be a rampaging toddler or dog on the loose. Whatever it is, children need a grown-up to step in from time to time, and you'll have to be ready and on the spot. Your role will vary (referee, security guard, cheerleader, consultant), depending on the particular drama that's unfolding, and your verbs will, too. If you're swift and sure to respond, children will know they can count on you. They'll also be less apt to take the administration of justice into their own hands, which is in no one's best interest.

A group of adults reading Scripture in the repertory church needs help occasionally, too. And let's face it: not every adult is a grown-up. When tempers flare and tensions build, or when the group's questions and dynamics have exceeded its capacity to handle them, it may be time to bring in a mediator: a grown-up mediator. This could be a pastor or a counselor, or some other wise and mature person the group trusts to be fair and impartial. It could also be a scholar, if the group needs more information on a matter of interpretation. If there's an issue, don't let it fester. Invite someone with another perspective to help sort it out.

– 8 –
Keep the neighborhood cats out of the sandbox.

This sandbox rule was suggested to me by some church ladies in Tennessee who plunged into the spirit of the exercise with great enthusiasm. Cats, they noted, are delightful creatures, but not in your child's sandbox. To a cat, every sandbox is a cat box waiting to happen. This is an obvious complication you will need to address, since children must have a clean and reasonably hygienic place to play, and cats have different ideas. Install some cat-repelling devices that will keep the sandbox filled with . . . sand.

I assume these ladies from Tennessee were so quick to contribute this particular rule because of some prior experience with a Bible study gone bad. Maybe they had witnessed one person dumping all over the group. Maybe they had seen how just a little toxicity can spoil the whole. Whatever the case, they were clear, and I agree with them: There isn't any room for cats when you're reading Scripture in the repertory church. We need a space that's safe for everyone to be, or at least as safe as we can make it. Decide together what your over-the-limit contamination quotas and verbs are.

– 9 –
What we build in sand doesn't last forever.

Sandcastles are as fleeting as a golden afternoon. They're not meant to endure for long. Overnight, the wind will blow and the rain will fall, and when you come back the next day, all that will remain of the child's labors is a small mound of sand. This is the way of things. This is the nature of sand and time, as God has created them. You can help the child to see the beauty in this, as well as her place in the order of things: the grass withers, the flowers fade, the castles fall back into the sand, but the Word of our God will stand forever. A sandbox is a child's introduction to the concept of mortality.

Readers of Scripture in every age know it: what we see in the text is ours for the day, and it speaks to us for the day that is ours. The Word is eternal; our interpretations are for a context. The Word is timeless; our readings are of their time. The verbs we recognize in the text today have likely been recognized before, and will be again. That is a mystery and a gift, and a freedom besides. We don't have to speak for all peoples in all places. We don't have to play the script as they would. We don't have to come up with an interpretation that endures. Only the Word endures. Every group just takes its turn to read it in the repertory church.

– 10 –

Come back tomorrow and build again.

A sandbox is an open invitation, a free season pass, and everyone gets one. Children know this in theory, but they won't remember it in practice. When it's time to give someone else a turn to dig in their spot, or time to pack up and leave the park for the day, they may be utterly bereft. There may be sobbing and wailing of biblical proportions, as if this leave-taking were permanent and even vindictive on your part. It's a normal reaction. Your job is to repeat the promise of grace: *The sandbox will be here tomorrow. We can come back. We can always come back. Tomorrow, you can build again.* And if the exchange sounds familiar to you, as if liturgical echoes or resonances were lingering in the air—well, then that's good for both of you. A sandbox gives a child a glimpse of grace. A child's longing for a sandbox gives an adult a glimpse of it, too.

Reading Scripture in the repertory church is an open invitation, too—for any group, any time. And every Bible comes with a free season pass. We can open it again and again, and each time be guaranteed a fresh start, a brand-new experience. There are plenty of places to sit, and buckets and shovels to go around. There are castles to build and time to build them. There are friends to share ideas with, or just to sit next to, as we quietly do our own work. Later, we can admire everyone's verbal prowess: what they have built, or built-and-demolished, since sometimes the ruins are as entertaining as the castles. Tomorrow, we can come back and build again. We can always build again. The sandbox of our Scripture, the *script* in our Scripture, is ready and waiting.

CHAPTER 6

Saying Something True

Six Questions to Lead Us from Reading to Speaking

The repertory church is an offshoot of the slow movement. If you're used to grabbing your Scripture on the run or at the drive-through window, you may have to adjust your speed settings a bit; this isn't reading you can do fast, on the fly. But it can be a real pleasure to slow down and take your time with the words, enjoying the local wildlife (or wild things) as you read the verbs and rehearse the text. It really is reading in a more connected way, at a grassroots level. And in the long run, it's more nourishing and sustainable for the local ecosystem than canned or processed readings. Maybe we've all had enough of factory-farmed Scripture and fast-food church.

So allow at least an hour to read and rehearse the text—longer, if the group has the time or inclination. Then everyone can take a break, and reconvene for the best part of all: saying something true.

You Saw Something. Say Something.

I might not have gotten interested in the out-loud dimension of reading and interpretation if I didn't have such a peculiar job. When you listen to people (seminary students) stammer their way to a deep truth (sermon) from their engagement with a text (Scripture), and you do this all day, you spend a lot of time being amazed—by your students' faith, courage, and remarkable insight. You watch them march straight into a biblical script without flinching and come back to say something true, and you begin to suspect that *reading* and *speaking* go hand in hand, since one appears to flow seamlessly into the other.

And then you think, How could more of us get in on the act? And wouldn't the repertory church be the logical place to do this? After all, it helps solitary readers become community readers. Could it create a community of speakers as well? Could the repertory church be a place where we turn our silent reading into speaking and performing and living the text—out in the world?

I believe it could! And that a few strategic questions can turn our *seeing* something into *saying* something. That's what you'll find in this chapter: six questions to let reading and speaking go hand in hand, one flowing seamlessly into the other. It's a process that's designed to be done in pairs, after your group has finished reading the verbs and rehearsing the text. Then you can come back together in the large group to share responses.

The six questions follow below, and you can watch how the responses build, one upon another. (For more details about group process, and further examples of how these six questions might play out in a repertory church group that's working with the same Genesis 3 text, see Appendices 4 and 5.)

Six Questions

– 1 –
What's the place in the text that gets you?

What this question is really asking is, "What's the place in the text that fascinates you, bothers you, troubles you, thrills you, haunts you, angers you, gladdens you, or otherwise jumps up to meet you?"—but that takes too long to say. "Gets you" will have to do. Yet as laid back and slangy as it sounds, you can hear the urgency underneath. You're looking for the moment in your reading and rehearsing *when you find the script in Scripture.*

That moment is one of recognition, yes, but it's also a moment of address. It's the Spirit trying to get your attention. I've lived in the Deep South long enough to write that with complete sincerity and absolutely no embarrassment. The place in the text that sticks to you, no matter how hard you try to shake it off, is the moment of encounter you must pay attention to; it is the seed of what you will say. Your job is not to ignore it, because if you do, it will just keep coming up, again and again, every chance it gets. (Ask a therapist how "denial" works.)

The Spirit is relentlessly persistent. It is also ridiculously accurate. *This is why texts get us* in particular ways, at particular times: the Spirit is matching the right address with the right speaker at the right moment for the right people. So pay attention. When, in your reading and rehearsing of this text, did you discover that certain verbs were making a big entrance and expecting an ovation? Were you immediately *engrossed* or *captivated* or *delighted* at some point? Did you find yourself unaccountably *bothered* or *puzzled* or *infuriated* by a detail? When the text elicits strong emotions, it's a good indicator that a script is bobbing into view, and it might well be yours. The script in Scripture usually comes with verbs that want to be the star of your show, whether you decided to cast them or not.

As you ask the "big entrance" question, take a mental inventory of what happened to you during the reading: what you saw and heard and felt. Identify the moment when your reaction to the text was the strongest, in whatever verb form that took. It probably won't take long. The Spirit isn't known for being especially subtle or reticent in these matters; when it starts banging you over the head with your own script, you can usually tell.

Match that moment with the exact place in the text: locate the verse, and read it out loud for your partner or the whole group. That announcement serves a few purposes. It reaffirms your choice, orients the ones who are listening (who have just encountered this very text with you), and often results in a chorus of empathetic nods and murmurs. Your group may not know how that verse got *you*, but they all know it's a verse that's perfectly capable of bulldozing a city block. It could have gotten any of them—and may in fact be the verse your partner chose, too!

Example: The place in the text that gets me is the last two verses: "But the LORD God called to the man and said to him, 'Where are you?' He said, 'I heard the sound of you in the garden, and I was afraid, because I was naked; and I hid myself'" (Gen. 3:9–10).

– 2 –
Why does it get you?

What this question is really asking is, *Why* does this moment in the text fascinate you, bother you, trouble you, thrill you, haunt you, anger you, gladden you, or otherwise jump up to meet you?—and that still takes too long to say. But the key word this time is "why." Why the strong reaction? Why does this moment awaken those verbs?

The response you're looking for, as you might guess, is simple: *Because this is a text I've played. That moment got me because I recognized the script in Scripture—and a few verbs I wasn't expecting made sure I wouldn't miss it.*

When you make the connection between the text and the script—or how the text has been *your* script—you're really acknowledging the work of the Spirit in its efforts to get your attention. It's a little like answering your phone after letting thirteen calls from the same number go straight to voicemail: you resign yourself to the fact that someone is determined to talk to you and is going to keep trying. But in the Spirit's case, these aren't random or trivial messages. They're moments of truth, and they'll lead to more truth. You answer them so that later you can offer them: come back and say something true from a script you know.

For example, maybe the exchange between the woman and the serpent gets you because you, too, have played verse 5. You recognize that slippery "when" clause ("*when* you eat this, you *will be* [. . .]!"), and how it once distracted you from the order in the garden. It isn't a time you're especially proud of. You don't feel the need to overshare. But you know the reason those verbs make you jump is because they once made you crawl.

Or maybe the man and woman hiding in the garden, in verse 8, is the place that gets you because you have a friend that's playing that script right now. Your friend has a passion for a certain ministry and a gift for leadership. Others have noticed this, including you, but your friend doesn't think she has the knowledge or experience to step up into a new role. She keeps downplaying her own abilities, even though everyone around her sees them plain as day. You hear the verb "hiding," and what you see is your friend, crouching in the underbrush—and you ache for her to hear God's voice, calling her to come out.

The "why" question is critical. It is for you to name for yourself: how the text has been your script. You don't have to tell anyone or reveal more than the group setting warrants, but you do have to know. You have to make the connection and move on. Then you can change the subject away from yourself, which is essential if you want to say something true *about God*, and not about your mother, your stepfather, your relationship woes or commitment issues. These things have a way of interfering with our reading and rehearsing if we're not clear about naming the script that's before us. And the Spirit has more in mind for you than a recitation of your personal history. Or a sublimation of it, for that matter—long harangues about all those shiny nouns because it was easier than dealing with the verbs you knew firsthand.

As you reflect, remember that this moment in the text is the Spirit's gift, not the serpent's. It's an invitation to blessing, not the opposite. Be encouraged—and be honest.

Example: The reason this moment in the text (verses 9–10) gets me is because God's question ("Where are you?") is one my friends and I began asking ourselves not long ago. We realized that if we want anything in this world to change, we have to get involved. We can't hide in a forest of apathy; we have to show up and be counted. And we have to believe we can make a difference, even if it's only in small ways. Somehow, it took that question—"Where are you?!"—to wake us up and get us moving.

– 3 –
What do you know about God from this moment in the text that gets you?

With this question, we change the subject back to God. That's been the aim all along: *We read and rehearse with the repertory church so we can say something true—something that matters vitally for the world—about God.* So, from playing this script, what do you know and believe about God? How would you express this in response to what the text has shown you—or not shown you?

For instance, the text may have lifted up the goodness and greatness of God's verbs, something you want to shout from the rooftops with joy. Maybe God's *calling* verb strikes you as central to who God is: that God calls us, and calls us out, whether we've fallen for the snake oil or are hiding among the trees. What you see in the text is that God wants to be in relationship with us, no matter what we do or where we are—and that God even initiates it! You believe this wholeheartedly. Now you want to come back and say something true about it.

Or the text may have shown you something else—that here, God's verbs left a lot to be desired. They weren't positive at all. They didn't inspire much joy or gratitude. If anything, they made you want to holler at God to get back in character, with more of those goodness-and-greatness verbs. What you see in the text is that God appears to have skipped town in the first half of this story, while the serpent was peddling its dope through the playground. What you know about God is that God is more than this: God shows up, sooner or later—as the big wide story of Scripture shows us—with verbs of love and care. And you want to come back and say something true about this, too.

The point is that this question is asking us to be utterly honest about *the picture of God this text is showing us*—and to respond to that picture with honest faith. We *say something true* about the God we have experienced here, even when it means coming clean about God's inexplicable absence or silence. And we *say something true* about the God we trust and wait for, who has promised to be with us. We let the broad sweep of Scripture have its say in our hearts. We call down God's verbs of love and care.

It's important to stress the "utterly honest" piece. Without it, we might revert back to all those solitary-reader tendencies. Reading head-first rather than feet-first. Keeping the text at a safe distance. Quoting doctrine we've read rather than doctrine we've experienced. Saying something true, but not necessarily a true thing we actually believe.

There are many ways to honor the text. But perhaps we honor it best with our honesty—when we say what we know about God, even when (and especially when) we've found the script in Scripture.

Example: I know God calls to us when we're hiding, and wants us to step up and say where we are: to name it, own it, admit it. And when we do, I believe God meets us with grace so we can live in the light—with truth, compassion, and justice.

– 4 –
Why does your community need to hear this today—what you know about God? Why is it important to tell them?

Now we move to the listeners, the ones who will hear these words. As you picture all that's going on in their lives and contexts, ask yourself why it's important for them to hear this—what you know about God from your encounter with this text. Why does it matter to them? Why does it matter today, right now?

This question helps us attend to issues of relevance and urgency. There's a lot of noise in the world. If what we say about God just adds to it, we might as well be quiet.

But if what we say matters vitally, if it speaks to the needs and concerns of real people in real places, people we love and care for, then we must speak up. It won't be noise. It will be a word about God in the script we're all playing.

One way to think about this question is to imagine your words as a gift. What do you want to give your community right now? And not just because it's what they *want* to hear. Because it's what they *need* to hear in the core of their being. To survive and thrive, they need to receive this word about God, and you're the one who can bring it to them—the one who loves them enough to say something true. It's a lot like the way relatives read your holiday and birthday wish lists when you're young. Sure, you want a jet ski. But you *need* a new belt and a wool sweater. Merry Christmas.

The point isn't that the sensible presents are always the boring ones, or the wish list always a pipe dream. A gift we need, or never even knew we lacked, can be life and breath. Words can be spirit and truth. Words about God can save in every way it's possible to save. And if they're offered as gift to our community rather than a dose of medicine, they will.

To offer this gift, we do have to love them. Otherwise, we're just correcting them. And that's no gift at all. It's coal in their stockings.

Example: My friends and I come from different faith backgrounds. It's pretty ingrained in us to keep religion separate from politics.

When we talk about what's motivated us to wake up and get moving, most of the reasons sound negative: we're outraged, incredulous, sobered, or scared. I think we could reframe these feelings positively if we drew on the resources of faith—that the biggest motivation for waking up is God's call to each of us, and God's vision for all of us. The biggest motivation is God, not the serpent! My friends and I need some empowering, common ground-building words, so we can all be moving *toward* something rather than running *away* from something.

– 5 –
What do you want to say?

This is your thesis statement, or "focus" (as Thomas G. Long so indelibly put it in *The Witness of Preaching*). If you can, say it in one sentence. Looking your partner in the eye.

It's a lot tougher to do than you might expect. After slogging through the first four questions, you'd think *this* one would be a breeze: happy trails from here on out. Actually, it's more like *miles to go before I sleep*—or seems so, when you're stumbling over words.

This is often the moment when you need the most encouragement from the group. When your head is swimming with all the insights you've garnered, returning to that essential moment—the one the Spirit was doing its best to dazzle you with—may be your very last instinct. You need others to remind you of where you started, and where it led, and the pillars of cloud and fire that are shimmering just ahead. Keep it simple. *God is the subject. We encountered God in this text. I have a word to speak, a word that matters, for people I love. This is what I want to say.*

If you come up blank, let your partner and perhaps the larger group prompt you. That's one of the great advantages of having witnesses when you respond to these questions: you may remember none of what you said ten seconds ago, but they will. You may despair at how slow of speech and slow of tongue you are, but they'll also help you through that Slough of Despond.

To your ears, your words may sound like garbled mishmash. To the group, they'll have the ring of truth—perhaps the very one they've been longing to hear.

Example: God's call to each of us and God's vision for all of us are why we are awake and alive in a new script, and we can claim that with joy, holding hands across traditions.

– 6 –
What do you hope these words will do?

This is the outcome statement, or "function" (in Long's words). If you can, say it in one sentence. Looking your partner in the eye.

We can never predict or control all that our words will do, of course. But intention is important. This question asks us to think seriously about that: since words do things to people, what do we hope *our* words will do? Have we framed them in a way that will help or hinder that? Do we need to reframe or rephrase? Have we attended carefully enough to our listeners in their contexts?

If you've ever gotten into a heated discussion with a friend or family member that started with some variation of "It's not what you said; it's how you said it!" or "I can't believe you'd be so insensitive as to bring that up *now*, of all times!," then you know what's at stake here: hurt feelings, ruffled feathers, hopping-mad spouse, long night. Reflecting on what our words may do (and what we hope they will do) tests whether what we are offering is truly a gift. Maybe what we want to say about God is really for our own benefit, rather than that of our listeners. Maybe it serves our needs rather than theirs. Maybe we haven't taken into full account all that's going on in their lives: what they're coping with, wrestling with, struggling with. If any of these are true, then the gift may have morphed into something akin to that awesome coffeemaker you give your roommate for her birthday when *you're* the one who drinks coffee.

This question asks us to consider the hospitality of our words: whether there's room for the other in what we'll say. Whether our words will open a door of welcome or guard a gated community. Whether they will set a place at the table—or make clear that we never intended to sit down and break bread with our listeners at all. They can always tell.

And the door we hope to open is the one that points to God.

Example: Whatever tradition we stand in, I hope these words will quietly empower us to see God as the good initiator of all our work and the prime inspiration for it.

Six Questions at Work in Your Group and Beyond

So, when it comes time for the community of readers to become a community of speakers, how can these six questions help us make the transition?

We might begin by acknowledging the obvious—that it *is* a transition, and we won't all approach it in the same way! Some of us find it easy and natural to talk about our faith; for others, it's an obstacle course. The reasons are as varied and complex as we are, and they don't always fall into neat patterns. Maybe we were raised in a faith tradition that encouraged speech—but not ours. Maybe we were allowed to say certain things about God—but not other things. Everything about us, from our disposition to our life experience, influences how we speak about God: when we speak, where, why, and with whom.

For this reason, your group might spend a few minutes sharing each person's history. It will help you to hear and encourage one another when it comes time to speak. Then you can change the subject from yourselves to God, and get back to what happened in your reading and rehearsing.

As you do, here are some ways to work with the six questions in this chapter.

– 1 –
Ask them with your group.

It takes courage to speak about God in front of others. It also takes patience, effort, and a lot of practice. Most of us are better at *saying anything* than *saying something true.* So a group is a great help in this regard, kind of like joining an exercise class and training together for a road race. You grumble a bit, stretch a bit, sweat a lot, and go a little farther each time. The workouts don't exactly get easier, but you get better at doing them. And you definitely do them better in the company of others, who are running the same race that you are.

The repertory church makes an excellent group exercise class. All the other verbs you might do at the gym—run, spin, lift, stretch, pump, dance, bend, and pose—you can do with Scripture, together, and it will help with the transition from reading to speaking. Even if you still like your solitary long walks (and reads), community reading will strengthen your saying-something-true muscles.

It's also important to remember something else about truth-telling: in this work, practice *doesn't* make perfect. Only God is perfect. Our words will never say all there is to say about God; frankly, they won't even come close. But we try, because it makes us more reverent, compassionate, tolerant, and faithful. So try together. Try, and be ready to fail, willing to fail, willing to get back up and try again, willing to lift one another up. When we let go of our need to be *right*, we may speak a word that is *true*.

– 2 –
Ask them with your faith community.

Faith communities value spiritual practices, and most of the faith communities I know are always looking for ways to help their people connect with meaningful ones. If your group finds joy in this or any other practice, spread the word. Invite others to join you. Offer to facilitate another group until it gets going. Suggest that your community read the verbs for a season. Even better, do it intergenerationally. Scripture reading in many communities tends to be an age-determined thing: youth read with youth; adults read with adults. Naturally, there are good reasons for this. But there are also good reasons for mixing it up and letting the particular wisdoms of each generation enrich the other. One of the reasons I love to practice those three R's (reading, rehearsing, and rumpus) in a large group setting is that there are usually many ages on hand, and twelve-year-olds and eighty-two-year-olds really do have some things to say to each other. Giving your faith community that experience—perhaps around a familiar, seasonal text—can be a powerful learning moment for everyone.

Faith communities also look for ways to get more people involved in worship. Some have many opportunities for this; others are searching for ways that fit. If your community creates space for people to offer a testimony or a brief reflection during the service, and if some are interested in speaking but not sure how to begin, this process might be a good one to consider: invite people to respond to a biblical text using the six questions as prompts. Alternatively, if your community incorporates small group discussion into the worship service, you might use the six questions as a template to guide your reflection. One benefit to this is that everyone gets to practice *speaking something true* on a regular basis; it becomes as natural as breathing. Another benefit is that everyone gets to *hear many true things, each one different, from the same text*, on a regular basis; that becomes as natural as breathing, too. Over time, it shapes the community to expect multiple readings and to welcome them. You may end up having a repertory church on your hands without even trying.

– 3 –
Ask them with the world.

Maybe human beings in every age have feared for the precariousness of their time. The biblical writers certainly did, and it's a formidable experience to read their apocalyptic visions for the end of the world. But something is different today. We all know it. We all feel it. And it isn't just the possibility of nuclear destruction or the certainty of climate change. It is our earth. Our ability to live with one another. Our ability to listen and talk across borders and politics and religious and racial differences. Our respect for truth and civility in public discourse. As I write this, "the cup of staggering" that Isaiah spoke of (51:22) is making the rounds, and we are all drinking from it.

If there was ever a time for a repertory church to step up, this is it. We have a vision of hope, and we have ways to speak of it, and those ways run counter to much of the speech in this world. What if the repertory church expanded the company of players? What if we read and rehearsed across traditions? What if we committed to ask one another six questions from our sacred texts, and to really hear and say something true as a community of readers, united in purpose? What if we read Scripture as if we believed it could save the world?

PART II

Encountering Scripture in the Repertory Church

CHAPTER 7

Asking New Questions

Reading and Rehearsing Mark 5

I spend a lot of time reading Mark. Do you find that you have a Gospel that you return to, over and over? For me, it's Mark. I'm not sure why: maybe it's the great teacher I had in seminary who helped me read it for the first time, or the students I had in class whose performance of it helped me hear it for the first time. Or maybe it's just that it's short: only sixteen chapters. I like an author who knows how to edit. Why say it in twenty-eight chapters (Matthew), or twenty-four (Luke), or twenty-one (John), if you can say it in sixteen? Mark is a model of brevity and restraint. If you want to improve your writing, read Mark.

Mark will also improve your reading and speaking in the repertory church. His words leap and sing and *land* somewhere, with a definite purpose. So every year, when it comes time to walk a class through the process of reading the verbs and rehearsing a text, I turn to Mark, chapter 5: the stories of the Gerasene demoniac, Jairus and his daughter, and the hemorrhaging woman. Every year it's a thrilling experience, and not just for those first-year students, who are starry-eyed. Some texts simply never get old, no matter how many times you read them. They always have a new word to speak. And they always inspire you to try and say it like Mark does: clearly, succinctly, and with abundant joy.

Some time ago, I decided to spend a year reading the fifth chapter of Mark with as many different groups as I could. I was thinking about verbs, and how all this rehearsing would translate beyond the classroom, and so I turned to a text I thought I knew inside and out. It seemed like a logical choice: I was current with the scholarship, I could recite the chapter by heart, and after nearly twenty years of reading it in a classroom of budding preachers, I knew where the pitfalls and best lookout spots were likely to be. I knew the sorts of questions to expect. I was ready! Right?

Not by a long stretch. What I forgot was one of the key rules of reading and rehearsing in the repertory church: *When the groups change, the questions change. And you can never assume that one group will ask all the questions that are possible and important to ask.*

No More Secrets

This became apparent almost immediately (which Mark would have liked). Right away, these repertory church reading and rehearsal groups started to ask questions that had never come up in my classroom—ever. I realized I'd been playing in the "preachers-only" end of the sandbox for way too long. The question I heard most often was this: *How come some people in Mark 5 get to tell about Jesus, and others don't?*

This wasn't a question my students and I had ever asked. In fact, it's not a question many preachers *would* ask—because we think we're supposed to know the answer, or at least the proper theories that would explain it. One of those, "The Messianic Secret," is a proposal put forth by nineteenth-century German scholar William Wrede to explain why, in Mark's Gospel, Jesus is always ordering people not to tell what they know about him. The theory is that Mark wants to keep Jesus's true identity a secret until the very end. No one will know until Jesus dies and is raised that he's the Messiah, because he's not the sort of Messiah everyone is expecting. He won't fight and win for us; he'll suffer and die for us. He'll die on a cross, which doesn't look very messianic on the face of things, but actually *is*, if you're in on the secret. Mark keeps delaying the fullness of who Jesus is until the very end, when we'll all be able to put the pieces together. That's the theory, and it's one most preachers have to learn in seminary.

So when these repertory church reading and rehearsal groups asked me, "How come some people get to tell about Jesus and others don't?", I naturally replied, "Well, that's 'The Messianic Secret.' It's this theory about the Gospel of Mark." And I explained it.

The repertory church people were so very patient. They listened politely, and then said, "Okay, we get the theory. 'Don't tell the secret until the end of the Gospel.' So why aren't the characters in the fifth chapter of Mark following the rule?"

"What do you mean?" I asked, startled.

"Well," they answered, "there's nothing secret in the fifth chapter of Mark! Everybody hears about Jesus, and a lot of people are talking about him."

"Maybe we should go back to Chapter 1 in Mark," I suggested. "You see? There's a story about Jesus healing a leper, and then he strictly orders the leper not to tell anyone. *That's* 'The Messianic Secret.'"

"Yeah," they said, "but look: the leper goes out and blabs anyway."

"True," I replied.

They pressed on. "And what about the demons and the unclean spirits? Mark says they know him. Jesus won't let them talk, but they know him, and it's not the end of the story yet!"

"Good point," I said.

"And what about Chapter 5?" they continued. "Why does the Gerasene demoniac get to tell what he knows about Jesus, and the leader of the synagogue, Jairus, whose little daughter was raised, doesn't? How come some characters get to talk and others don't?"

And suddenly it hit me. Maybe my preachers-only groups had been asking the wrong question. Maybe the issue isn't *what* we're supposed to tell, or *when* we're supposed to tell it. Maybe it's *who* gets to tell. And you know who gets to tell about Jesus in Chapter 5? Crazy people and twelve-year-old girls, and a woman who hemorrhages her whole truth in front of God and everybody.

Let's take a good look at that chapter. Here, as elsewhere, I'll be using the NRSV translation (with a few pronoun edits, here and there, for clarity and inclusivity):

MARK, CHAPTER 5

1 They came to the other side of the sea, to the country of
the Gerasenes. 2 And when Jesus had stepped out of the
boat, immediately a man out of the tombs with an unclean
spirit met him. 3 The man lived among the tombs; and no
one could restrain him anymore, even with a chain; 4 for
he had often been restrained with shackles and chains, but
the chains he wrenched apart, and the shackles he broke in
pieces; and no one had the strength to subdue him. 5 Night
and day among the tombs and on the mountains he was

always howling and bruising himself with stones. 6 When the man saw Jesus from a distance, he ran and bowed down before him; 7 and he shouted at the top of his voice, "What have you to do with me, Jesus, Son of the Most High God? I adjure you by God, do not torment me." 8 For Jesus had said to him, "Come out of the man, you unclean spirit!" 9 Then Jesus asked him, "What is your name?" The man replied, "My name is Legion; for we are many." 10 He begged him earnestly not to send them out of the country. 11 Now there on the hillside a great herd of swine was feeding; 12 and the unclean spirits begged him, "Send us into the swine; let us enter them." 13 So Jesus gave them permission. And the unclean spirits came out and entered the swine; and the herd, numbering about two thousand, rushed down the steep bank into the sea, and were drowned in the sea.

14 The swineherds ran off and told it in the city and in the country. Then people came to see what it was that had happened. 15 They came to Jesus and saw the demoniac sitting there, clothed and in his right mind, the very man who had had the legion; and they were afraid. 16 Those who had seen what had happened to the demoniac and to the swine reported it. 17 Then they began to beg Jesus to leave their neighborhood. 18 As he was getting into the boat, the man who had been possessed by demons begged him that he might be with him. 19 But Jesus refused, and said to him, "Go home to your friends, and tell them how much the Lord has done for you, and what mercy he has shown you." 20 And the man went away and began to proclaim in the Decapolis how much Jesus had done for him; and everyone was amazed.

[21] When Jesus had crossed again in the boat to the other side, a great crowd gathered around him; and he was by the sea. [22] Then one of the leaders of the synagogue named Jairus came and, when he saw him, fell at his feet [23] and begged him repeatedly, "My little daughter is at the point of death. Come and lay your hands on her, so that she may be made well, and live." [24] So Jesus went with him.

And a large crowd followed him and pressed in on him. [25] Now there was a woman who had been suffering from hemorrhages for twelve years. [26] She had endured much under many physicians, and had spent all that she had; and she was no better, but rather grew worse. [27] She had heard about Jesus, and came up behind him in the crowd and touched his cloak, [28] for she said, "If I but touch his clothes, I will be made well." [29] Immediately her hemorrhage stopped; and she felt in her body that she was healed of her disease. [30] Immediately aware that power had gone forth from him, Jesus turned about in the crowd and said, "Who touched my clothes?" [31] And his disciples said to him, "You see the crowd pressing in on you; how can you say, 'Who touched me?'" [32] Jesus looked all around to see who had done it. [33] But the woman, knowing what had happened to her, came in fear and trembling, fell down before him, and told him the whole truth. [34] He said to her, "Daughter, your faith has made you well; go in peace, and be healed of your disease."

[35] While he was still speaking, some people came from the leader's house to say, "Your daughter is dead. Why trouble the teacher any further?" [36] But overhearing what they said, Jesus said to the leader of the synagogue, "Do not fear,

> only believe." 37 He allowed no one to follow him except
> Peter, James, and John, the brother of James. 38 When they
> came to the house of the leader of the synagogue, he saw a
> commotion, people weeping and wailing loudly. 39 When
> he had entered, he said to them, "Why do you make a
> commotion and weep? The child is not dead but sleeping."
> 40 And they laughed at him. Then he put them all outside,
> and took the child's father and mother and those who were
> with him, and went in where the child was. 41 He took her
> by the hand and said to her, "Talitha cum," which means,
> "Little girl, get up!" 42 And immediately the girl got up and
> began to walk about (she was twelve years of age). At this
> they were overcome with amazement. 43 He strictly ordered
> them that no one should know this, and told them to give
> her something to eat.

Who Gets the Power to Speak?

Here's what I learned, the year I left the preachers-only sandbox and started reading Mark 5 with the repertory church. I learned that when I'm not looking for a sermon, I actually hear a text differently. I'm not trying out focus and function statements to find something (anything) that fits. I'm not worried about what I'm going to say in exactly thirty-six hours. I don't have any of that pressure at all. I can just listen to Mark speak in the company of other interested listeners. If the text is awkward—well, then, it's awkward. I can ask questions. If I don't like the answers, I can keep pressing, because it's not my job to explain anything; I'm just reading. And that lets me get interested in details I might otherwise rush past if I have a deadline. It lets me ask different sorts of questions, the kind that preachers don't ever seem to ask.

I had been reading Mark 5 with preachers for years, and not one of us had ever asked about that Gerasene demoniac, why he gets to talk, and Jairus doesn't. It wasn't because we weren't smart enough or schooled enough or diligent enough—or even, for an eight a.m. class, awake enough. I think we never asked that question because we were preparing to be the ones who *do* get to talk about Jesus, and *it wasn't in our interests to ask it.*

It's a funny thing: the church gives preachers the power to speak, but in Scripture, it's different. In Scripture, the one who has the power to speak isn't always the leader of the synagogue. It's the marginalized person, the crazy person, the teenager you've given up for dead. And while you would certainly offer hospitality to a demoniac by inviting him to worship, *this* text suggests you invite him into the pulpit, too.

When churches are shrinking and sermons are suspect, when preachers find it harder and harder to gain a hearing in a culture that has little time or interest, the "power to speak" isn't what it used to be. Most preachers aren't exactly looking to identify with twelve-year-olds and demoniacs, as Scripture might have them do.

But speaking about Jesus isn't just for those who know the password and can access the data. That's a pretty dangerous road to go down these days—the road where some of us are in on a secret and others aren't. The road where those with superior knowledge have authority and others don't. In the big wide church, that road can lead to disaster. The moment a preacher's speech becomes primarily about *preserving* the power to speak, because of secret and superior knowledge, then we need an intervention.

And that's exactly what these repertory church reading groups were—a saving intervention! In the repertory church, we're all equal partners in reading the verbs. We need one another to rehearse the text. We thrive on asking new questions and exploring the angles. No one has to "own" the secrets, or reveal the password, or shoulder the entire burden of saying something true. The fifth chapter of Mark, as the repertory church showed me, is a brilliant place to look for new role models. Four characters show us what the power to speak looks like. And that's very good news for everyone who wants to speak about Jesus.

The Gerasene Demoniac

The first person we meet in this story is the Gerasene demoniac, or perhaps we should say "the man formerly known as the Gerasene demoniac," since Jesus heals him. But he never asked for it. He was perfectly content in his own graveyard, listening to his own voices, chunking away at his own chains. Who needs to be clothed and in your right mind when no one can subdue you? For Jesus, it must have been a great publicity opportunity. Cast the demons out of the crazy guy in the graveyard, and Jesus can make a name for himself. People are going to notice something's different in the neighborhood, especially if he does that cliff-jumping thing with the swine at the end: nice touch. It will be all over the evening news.

The problem is that people don't always like to see a change in their neighborhood. *You mean you're taking away our demoniac? What will we show the tourists now? This is what we're known for in Gerasene country—our haunted graveyard and shackled lunatic! He was our one reliable scapegoat, and now he and his legion are gone?*

Get this stranger out of here, before he ruins any more real estate or drowns any more herds! And Mark says the villagers begged Jesus to leave the neighborhood.

If Jesus wasn't welcome in this town, the man formerly known as the demoniac obviously sensed that he wasn't, either, and begged Jesus to allow him to come along. Jesus wouldn't do that, but he did give the man a new verb: *tell.* "Go home to your friends," Jesus said, "and tell them how much the Lord has done for you, and what mercy he has shown you."

There are several strange things about this. One is Jesus's assumption that the man has a home and friends, when the villagers have clearly indicated that he doesn't. Another is that the man has a story to tell that people will (first) want to hear, and (second) believe. This isn't mission territory that strikes one as particularly hospitable for a new church plant.

But Jesus doesn't worry about whether it's fertile ground or not. He doesn't stop to ask if the man seems particularly suited to his new verb. He doesn't review any credentials or request audition tapes. Jesus simply sends him out to tell the story. "Go home. Tell your friends. Tell them what the Lord did for you, before you ever knew to ask. Tell them he showed you mercy before you ever knew what it was. Tell them, *Once I lived in a tomb, and was possessed by demons. Now I live in freedom, and am possessed by grace.* It's a good story, and it's yours! So tell it."

Jairus and His Daughter

The next characters we meet in Mark's text are Jairus and his daughter. She's twelve years old and on her deathbed. He's a leader of the synagogue and out of options. The reports about the rabbi from Nazareth, and the verbs he was capable of—*heal* and *cure*—must have reached Jairus's ears and been his last hope for his child. He was desperate enough to throw himself at Jesus's feet, in front of the whole town, and beg for help: "My little daughter is at the point of death," he pleaded. "Come and lay your hands on her, so that she may be made well, and live." It's a public scene with frantic imperatives that everyone gets to witness. And whether Jesus is moved by the girl's plight or the father's anguish, he goes, without saying a word.

They're interrupted on the way to the house, which we'll get to in a minute. Suffice it to say that the interruption takes time—too much time, as far as the girl is concerned. She dies before they reach her bedside. And when the news is brought to them, Jesus quickly turns to Jairus with two of the most maddeningly cryptic, unbearably open-ended imperatives a holy man or a Jedi master can utter: "Do not fear; only believe."

Do not fear *what*?—that she's dead? Only believe *what*?—that Jesus can raise her? How you finish the sentence makes all the difference, as anyone who has ever agonized over what to pray for knows, but Jesus doesn't give Jairus any concrete guidance on what that ending might be. He lets Jairus work it out on his own, sounding a lot like Yoda in the process. And now we have a huge collision of worlds coming, because in Jairus's world, death *is* the end. Dead is dead and it *stays* dead—and why pray for miracle verbs that will only be torture to imagine? Why ask for impossible endings, verbs like "resurrect," when, up to this point in Mark's Gospel, Jesus himself has never raised the dead?

Jesus's enigmatic streak continues when they arrive at the leader's house and meet the mourners. "Why do you make a commotion and weep?" he asks them, as if they had somehow gotten the wrong address, and the bereavement was supposed to be happening three doors down. "The child is not dead but sleeping." The mourners find this hilarious—for a moment, they forget they're supposed to be *weeping and wailing loudly*—but Jesus firmly dismisses them and heads inside. He takes only a small group of witnesses with him: the girl's parents, Peter, James, and John. And then, as if he were finally getting around to that *heal* verb that Jairus originally begged him for, rather than the miracle verb that is now required, he takes the child by the hand and says, "Little girl, get up!" As if this isn't a resurrection at all. As if she isn't really dead, but sleeping—and way too late on a Saturday morning.

Of course she gets up immediately and begins to walk about. Twelve-year-old girls can *move*, and they're very busy people: things to do, places to go, people to meet. In an instant, she's off to meet the day. And Jesus tells the adults, who are standing around dumbstruck, that they're not to breathe a word of this to anyone; in fact, he strictly orders them *that no one should know this.* Instead, he suggests they give her something to eat. Maybe pancakes? Or would grilled cheese hit the spot?

The Hemorrhaging Woman

Now we return to that interruption, the one that delayed Jesus's progress to the house of Jairus. Mark introduces us to a fourth character, sandwiched in the middle of this chapter: not a leading citizen of the town or infamous local celebrity, but a person who has faded back to the sidelines. We call her the hemorrhaging woman, since we never learn her name.

This woman has been thrown a ghastly set of verbs that have bled her dry. *Suffering* from hemorrhages for twelve long years. *Endured* much under many physicians. *Spent all*, every cent that she had. *Was* no better. Rather, *grew worse*. It's just about the bleakest description of a life draining away that you'll ever find: a hemorrhaging of blood and hope, slow and cruel. Jairus was desperate, too; he tore through the crowd and threw himself at Jesus's feet. This woman couldn't even do that. She came up behind Jesus in the crowd, quietly, not to trouble or beg him for anything, but just to *touch* his cloak—because maybe one small verb is all you can manage when you're that depleted. Slip in, slip out. Hope that whatever jolt you get will be enough to heal you. Hope that maybe then, you'll remember how to live. "If I but touch his clothes," she said to herself, "I will be made well."

The moment she does, two things happen immediately. The first is that her hemorrhage abruptly stops. The second is that Jesus senses that someone has accessed his power current and plugged in to charge up. "Who touched me?" he asks, looking around for the one holding the charger. It's another of Jesus's more puzzling moments that can drive you up a wall, with questions about *omniscience* and *omnipotence*—whether Jesus knew all along who had touched him, or whether he permitted access to his power supply, or whether he even had control of his own voltage. And you'll probably have to bracket them, since there's no way Mark is going to let you resolve any of it neatly. No one leaves this passage without some serious dents in their Christological vehicle; after Mark 5, whatever you thought you knew about Jesus will need an overhaul. But if you can live in the tension and handle a few dings in your system, Mark invites you to go deeper than *a consistent truth*. He wants you to ponder *the whole truth*.

When Jesus spins about in the crowd, asking "Who touched me?" to all within reach and earshot, the woman responds in a remarkable way. She doesn't simply tell Jesus the truth. She tells him *the whole truth*: every single verb. She falls down in front of him and pours out the story of her hemorrhaged life—torrents of hurt and pain and longing that led to years of hiding, useless fig leaves. She steps up and names where she is. She tells him *who* she is, and how she got there, and why she dared to dream of more for herself than a ruptured existence. It's just as public as the leader of the synagogue's prostrations, but a good deal more perilous. Jairus only had his reputation as a Dignified Person to worry about. She has the weight and fury of purity laws raining down on her. If anyone wants to make an issue of the fact that *she touched a man*, they can, and this could turn into a public stoning.

But it doesn't. Jesus lets her speak her whole truth, without interruption or prompt. Jairus may be waiting, but the woman's moment holds his full attention—and the crowd's, too. They hear every word. They watch her wring out every last verb. And when she has finally finished telling her story in this very open forum, which we can only imagine was an unearthly mix of terror, embarrassment, and relief, Jesus lets her go with a blessing. "Daughter, your faith has made you well," he tells her, putting the crowd on notice. "Go in peace and be healed of your disease." He might as well have said, "Look, people: she's yours now. She's a daughter of Israel, and you've heard her story. Now treat her like family."

Back to the Question: So Who Gets to Speak?

And now we're back to our original question posed by the repertory church. Why does the Gerasene demoniac get to tell what he knows about Jesus, and Jairus doesn't?

These men actually have more in common than you might think. They each have a great story to tell. They're both public figures in their separate villages. Everyone knows that the Gerasene man was the notorious fellow who was crazy-possessed and lived in the graveyard until he was healed; they all saw it. Likewise, everyone knows that Jairus is a leader of the synagogue whose daughter was once so sick that she almost died—and maybe did; they all saw that, too. Two unbelievable stories of recovery, in every sense of that word. Two spellbinding stories of miracle cures.

Yet Jesus only allows the marginal man with a scandalous reputation to tell what the Lord has done for him. Jairus, the religious leader with a perfectly respectable reputation, is ordered to say nothing. And "reputation"—how we define it, assess it, assign it—seems to be at the heart of it.

If your authority comes from *who you are* rather than *what you know about Jesus*, that's a dangerous situation and a dangerous road. Jairus, had he been given free rein to talk, might have been tempted to tell a story about himself. He might have put himself at the center, in the starring role: "Yes, that's exactly what happened. I begged Jesus to come lay hands on my daughter, and he did. In fact, he brought her back from the dead! I was worried we might be too late, but he told me, 'Don't you be afraid, Jairus; only believe!'—and obviously I did, and it worked, because here she is, good as new! See what can happen if you just believe, like I do?!" And before you know it, Jairus has his own agent, his own book contract, his own regular news spot, and his own 10,000-member synagogue, because we all want to be like Jairus. We all want to read his bestseller, *The Prayer of Jairus*. *He's* the subject. And you can be too, if you buy his book and learn the seven habits of highly effective praying. . . .

But if Jairus doesn't get to speak, if Jesus orders him not to, then what happens? His daughter will go to the kitchen, get that grilled cheese sandwich, drink a glass of milk, eventually head outside to find her friends—and run straight into the crowd of mourners and gawkers, who are still wondering if there's going to be a funeral. They'll take one look at her and totally freak out; they'll literally lose their verbs. The ones who were weeping and wailing and then laughing and scoffing will now be hysterical, because what in the world is going on here? This daughter of Jairus was dead and is alive again—*Jesus,* what did you *do*? What should *we* do? Celebrate? Kill the fatted calf? Lock up the swine? Run for the hills?

If Jairus doesn't get to speak, then his daughter gets to tell *her* story. She'll tell it with her body, simply by being alive and well. And as she lives, which is all her father ever asked for her in the first place, she may find words to say a few things. She might smile at those mourners in their verb-disordered confusion and say, "All I know is this: I heard Jesus's voice calling me, and I felt his hand pulling me to my feet. So I got up and walked, and hugged my parents and ate, and here I am. Who's ready to play Capture the Flag?"

The testimony of a twelve-year-old girl may not sound like a dense theological treatise. But it's richer than any sermon preached because it is her life. And what she knows is this: *Jesus called her; Jesus took her by the hand; Jesus pulled her up*. That's all any of us want, isn't it?—to be that loved, that important, that wanted. If every twelve-year-old girl could preach that sermon, the world would be a different place. So let her speak it. Let her speak what she knows, even if she never uses words.

The Power to Speak You Give Away

So there you have it: four possibilities for speaking about Jesus, courtesy of the fifth chapter of Mark, where the primary question isn't *what* we say about Jesus—whether it coheres with a theory or a doctrine or some secret knowledge about Jesus's true identity. It isn't *what* we say, or *when*. It's *who* gets to say it: *who is allowed to speak*.

Here is Mark's take on that: *You are*. And you might not have to wait until the end of the story to open your mouth. You can speak from smack in the middle of your own life, exactly where you are. Because the only authority you have, the only power to speak you hold, comes from what you have seen and what you believe about Jesus. It won't come from superior knowledge, or secret passwords, or dent-free Christologies in showroom condition. It will come from where you meet Jesus in this text and in this life, every week, over and over again. That's such good news for a repertory church! It keeps us eager to read together, rehearse together, encounter God together—dents and dings and all—and share what we've seen and heard with our words and our lives. We won't own the text. We'll live it.

Mark gives us three scripts to practice all this. They aren't exactly role models. They are roles we will all get to play.

The first is the Hemorrhaging Speaker. This speech is a soliloquy: you offer it to God alone. You play it first, before you ever speak to others, because you can't tell anyone the truth about God unless you've told God the truth about you. Not just the truth; *the whole truth*. The places where you're losing blood and strength and hope for the world. The places you've tried to fix yourself and just can't, no matter how much you spend. It prepares you to tell your faith community the whole truth about God. And yes, it's a hard script to play, but you can do it; Jesus is turning about in the crowd, and you have his attention.

The second role is the Crazy-Possessed Speaker. This is the script you play every day, out in the world, every time you speak to others about God. Did you think you had the power to speak because you were a respectable person, a leader of the synagogue, and a treasured member of the repertory church? Think again. The minute you open your mouth to speak about Jesus, the world already knows you're fringe material. You're the person others see as not clothed and not in your right mind—and that's why Jesus chose you. He knew nobody would believe you because of *you*; they'd only believe you because it's a really good story. So tell it! *This is what the Lord did for us before we ever asked. This is the mercy of God: that we call one another friend, and lay down our lives.*

The third role is the Twelve-Year-Old Girl. This is the script you give away to others so they can speak about Jesus, too. You'll know who needs to play it: the ones who used to be dead and are alive again. The ones we gave up on but who somehow heard Jesus's voice. The ones who might be content to stay quiet because there are others who would be happy to tell their story for them—Jairus, for instance. But this isn't Jairus's role. It's not his story to tell. Jesus didn't raise that twelve-year-old girl because she's the child of Jairus. He raised her because she's a child of God. He raised her that she might be made well and live—and her story will unfold in the living. So give this script to the ones who need to play it, and encourage them to tell the story in their own way.

In this book I've spent a lot of time dwelling on *the script in Scripture* because the repertory church taught me it was there. I had to leave my own sandbox, and the ones I had grown comfortable digging with, to learn some old lessons: that our speaking to one another is only as powerful as our reading with one another. And a consistent truth is not the whole truth. And when the repertory church gathers, a text we think we know inside out and upside down will always surprise us with new questions. How can it not, with all those scripts to play? How can we resist, when Jesus wants to meet us in each one of them?

CHAPTER 8

Staying in the Scene

Reading and Rehearsing 2 Samuel 13

In 1982, Dr. Phyllis Trible, the ground-breaking feminist biblical scholar, was the first woman invited to give the Lyman Beecher Lectures on Preaching at Yale. She went down to the dusty archives of Scripture, hauled up three stories that nobody liked and nobody wanted, set them down in front of her listeners, and told them, *We're going in. Everyone, follow me.*

They did. And since Professor Trible knows how to plant her feet in a biblical text and doesn't scare easily, they followed her so far in that it's likely some of them needed oxygen masks. The title of those three Beecher lectures—"Texts of Terror: Unpreached Stories of Faith"—let many in the audience know that they'd been falling down on their primary verb and were about to have a performance review. When necessary, lectures on preaching must point out what pastors are *not* preaching.

The lectures were later published as *Texts of Terror,* which became an instant classic. Today, it's still sending shock waves through classrooms. The book is a companion to Trible's first landmark work, *God and the Rhetoric of Sexuality*, which contains literary feminist readings of stories about women in the Old Testament, the Hebrew Bible. While her first book is celebratory, *Texts of Terror* is sobering: it digs into the underbelly of Scripture, examining four often overlooked stories of women. These women—Hagar, Tamar, an unnamed concubine, and the daughter of Jephthah—have suffered unspeakable violence at the hands of men, including sexual abuse, assault, torture, incest, rape, murder, and sexual slavery. The book is a lament, a crying-out, and a call to repentance, because Trible is clear that while these stories are ancient and biblical, they're also happening in our streets and homes and churches every day.

Several decades have passed, and we continue to learn from Trible's work. We've also learned this: *The hardest part about reading hard texts is opening them—and staying in the scene*. How many have taken Trible's performance review to heart and actually read and rehearsed these texts so we can say something true? Not as many as we might hope for, and really, we haven't had much encouragement. None of these texts is in the lectionary. As far as the ecumenical councils are concerned, we can leave them alone, keep our distance, and the liturgical police will never cite us for gross negligence of Scripture.

This means that if you really want to read and rehearse a text of terror in the repertory church, you and your group have to go rogue: take the initiative, grit your teeth, adjust your oxygen masks, and launch into it. And obviously you'll have some terrible nouns to deal with—all those I just mentioned above. You and your group will have to talk about them, since that's what the stories are about, right? What else are you going to do with them but talk about the issues they raise?

The problem is that sly little preposition *about*, the one that circles and hops and never quite lands. That preposition can kill a reading. We can't talk *about* a text. We can talk about the issues it raises, yes, and indeed we must talk about the ones 2 Samuel 13 raises—learn about them, fight against them, work and pray to end them—but we can't talk *about* a text. Scripture is a living Word and an open script. We have to *enter* it, with the repertory church, the community of interpretation, walking beside us. We have to enter it and then stay in the scene. Otherwise, the text is just something we hold at arm's length and an appropriate distance. It's just a relic of antiquity to be exegeted by noted experts, visited with a seasoned tour guide like Trible, and then shut back into the pages of a library book.

But I don't believe that this is what Trible or most other Bible scholars intend for us. We *do* have an interpretive role—one that no one else can take for us. It isn't to shake our heads over the terrible nouns in a text. It's to rehearse the verbs the text offers us, which in this case are much more open-ended and one-size-fits-most than you might have guessed.

Pretend.
Would not listen.
Send in.
Send out.
Take hold.
Force.
Bolt the door.
Tear.
Cry aloud.
Keep quiet.
Speak neither good nor bad.
Remain.
Hate.

These are verbs I know. I wish I didn't, sometimes, but I do—and I remember the scripts. So now I don't have the option of distancing or dissociating myself with a nouns-first reading, and various sorts of literalism, such as "How can I speak *about* this text when those awful nouns—rape, abuse, assault, and the rest—aren't part of my experience?" I've just *had* an experience, caught in the headlights of the text's verbs. And that may have blessed and charged me with a word to speak.

What would happen if we walked into a text of terror as boldly as we do any other text and said, *We're going in—and we're not leaving until we've figured out which verbs are ours. Because the question isn't whether this text names our experience. The question is what experience emerges when we read this text together.*

What if we were brave enough to read hard stories—and brave enough to *stay in the scene*—until we found the script in Scripture, and a true word to say?

Reading 2 Samuel 13:1–22

In this chapter, we're going to read a text of terror, one of the four in Trible's book: the rape of Tamar in 2 Samuel 13:1–22. It's a story I've been reading for many years with groups around the country and abroad; it's also one of the first texts that I read with my students. I don't do it to make them miserable. We read it together so they'll know that *there's nothing they can't look at* in Scripture or in our world; and *there's no place, no crevice of our human life, that the Word of God can't go*; and when they read Scripture with the repertory church, *there's nothing that can separate them from the love of God in Christ Jesus—not even this text.*

I'm including the story below. Ordinarily, for a rehearsal reading, we'd go through every verb in the passage; here, we'll be selective and only venture into a few. In particular, we'll focus our attention on places in the text *where the story could have gone differently*. We'll ask what might have happened if someone had chosen a different verb.

A word of caution: this isn't a pretty story. It stirs deep emotions and can be traumatic to read. Since statistics tell us that one in four girls and one in six boys will be sexually abused by the age of eighteen (in the United States; in other countries, the numbers can be even higher), a good portion of us as readers will be connecting with some hard verbs very quickly. We'll need the compassion and tenderness of the repertory church as we read—because *texts do things to people. The world does things to people.* While it may be painful to see (as some of the male students in my class fumed one year, "You made us read this story, and we don't like seeing what it does to our sisters!"), that's our job, as people of faith: to see. And then to ask: What will we do with what we see?

2 SAMUEL 13

1 Some time passed. David's son Absalom had a beautiful
sister whose name was Tamar; and David's son Amnon fell
in love with her. 2 Amnon was so tormented that he made
himself ill because of his sister Tamar, for she was a virgin
and it seemed impossible to Amnon to do anything to her.
3 But Amnon had a friend whose name was Jonadab, the
son of David's brother Shimeah; and Jonadab was a very
crafty man. 4 He said to him, "O son of the king, why are
you so haggard morning after morning? Will you not tell

me?" Amnon said to him, "I love Tamar, my brother Absalom's sister." 5 Jonadab said to him, "Lie down on your bed,
and pretend to be ill; and when your father comes to see
you, say to him, 'Let my sister Tamar come and give me
something to eat, and prepare the food in my sight, so that I
may see it and eat it from her hand.'" 6 So Amnon lay down,
and pretended to be ill; and when the king came to see him,
Amnon said to the king, "Please let my sister Tamar come
and make a couple of cakes in my sight, so that I may eat
from her hand."

7 Then David sent home to Tamar, saying, "Go to your
brother Amnon's house, and prepare food for him." 8 So
Tamar went to her brother Amnon's house, where he was
lying down. She took dough, kneaded it, made cakes in his
sight, and baked the cakes. 9 Then she took the pan and set
them out before him, but he refused to eat. Amnon said,
"Send out everyone from me." So everyone went out from
him. 10 Then Amnon said to Tamar, "Bring the food into
the chamber, so that I may eat from your hand." So Tamar
took the cakes she had made, and brought them into the
chamber to Amnon her brother. 11 But when she brought
them near him to eat, he took hold of her, and said to her,
"Come, lie with me, my sister." 12 She answered him, "No,
my brother, do not force me; for such a thing is not done in
Israel; do not do anything so vile! 13 As for me, where could
I carry my shame? And as for you, you would be as one of
the scoundrels in Israel. Now therefore, I beg you, speak to
the king; for he will not withhold me from you." 14 But he
would not listen to her; and being stronger than she was,
he forced her and lay with her.

> 15 Then Amnon was seized with a very great loathing for her; indeed, his loathing was even greater than the lust he had felt for her. Amnon said to her, "Get out!" 16 But she said to him, "No, my brother; for this wrong in sending me away is greater than the other that you did to me." But he would not listen to her. 17 He called the young man who served him and said, "Put this woman out of my presence, and bolt the door after her." 18 (Now she was wearing a long robe with sleeves; for this is how the virgin daughters of the king were clothed in earlier times.) So his servant put her out, and bolted the door after her. 19 But Tamar put ashes on her head, and tore the long robe that she was wearing; she put her hand on her head, and went away, crying aloud as she went.
>
> 20 Her brother Absalom said to her, "Has Amnon your brother been with you? Be quiet for now, my sister; he is your brother; do not take this to heart." So Tamar remained, a desolate woman, in her brother Absalom's house. 21 When King David heard of all these things, he became very angry, but he would not punish his son Amnon, because he loved him, for he was his firstborn. 22 But Absalom spoke to Amnon neither good nor bad; for Absalom hated Amnon, because he had raped his sister Tamar.

The Setup

We begin with a short sentence: *Some time passed.* It's a signal that we're entering a story mid-progress: the lights are already dimmed, the projector is going, and we're tiptoeing down the aisle, twenty-five minutes into the movie. If we don't find out what we've missed, the rest of the action will never quite make sense. In this case, what we've missed is the story of David and Bathsheba in the previous two chapters. That blockbuster tale is frequently and bizarrely billed as one of the great romantic love stories of Scripture, but I'm not counseling my sons or yours to begin their relationships this way.

The plot to catch up on is that David has returned from war, victorious, and is now directing his troops from the palace; they're out of binocular range, but his gaze is still trained in multiple directions. One afternoon David lies down for a nap, wakes up, looks out the window, sees a beautiful woman bathing, and thinks—*I want that*. Let us note that he has several wives and many concubines at this point. There are, we might say, other options. But he's zeroed in, and he wants what he wants—even though the woman has a husband and isn't available.

David sees, wants, and takes. Why? *Because he can*. Because he's the king and has the power to do it.

This is exactly what the prophet Samuel warned about when Israel started wheedling for a king: kings, he cautioned, are dangerous. Even a king as golden and righteous as David is dangerous. Kings succumb to the temptation of their own power, and eventually they overstep. They take what doesn't belong to them; they take verbs that don't belong to them. They may even take life-and-death verbs that belong to God alone. And sure enough, that's what David does. There's a scandal—Bathsheba becomes pregnant—and the cover-up includes her husband's killing. Even though the prophet Nathan calls David out on it, the king still gets what he wants in the end: the woman, Bathsheba, who never speaks a single word in the entire story.

Those are the first twenty-five minutes of plot we're catching up on, with "some time passed": the long shadow of a royal scandal. Who do you think is watching the king during this entire escapade? His offspring. Children are always watching their parents, and as my sons often remind me, "Mom, we notice everything." They learn from our verbs. David's sons are watching: Amnon, the firstborn, and Absalom, the third son by another mother. His daughter is watching, too: Tamar, Absalom's sister. They all know what happened: *Dad wanted and took, because he could—and he got away with it.* And we might as well cue the ominous music, because there's a predatory precedent on the loose now, and the ones who are the most susceptible and vulnerable to it are David's family.

It Could Have Gone Differently: Friends' Verbs

We can see it prowling as soon as the story continues. Here's where we'll begin to catch sight of the verbs that nobody had control over, and the verbs that were absolutely within their control—the ones that could have gone differently. Plant your feet.

The crown prince gets the first fastball, which he handles in a worrisome way. *David's son Absalom had a beautiful sister whose name was Tamar; and David's son Amnon fell in love with her*. "Fell in love" is the verb he couldn't control, and the phrase itself underscores that. To say that we "fall" in love makes it sound like the verb was an accident, something we never meant to happen (you were just minding your own business, it was there, you tripped, and *boom*, you fell in it: "love"). And that's oddly accurate. No one plans this verb. You don't wake up one morning and announce, "Today, I will fall in love." You just go down, without warning. *Amnon fell in love*, and we can understand that this is the way of human beings: a verb beyond our control. But the problem here is that he fell for his half-sister, Tamar, who was off-limits. He fell in love with the wrong person. And what happened next *was* within his control.

But before we rush in to castigate Amnon, let's pause to consider that script—*falling in love with the wrong person*—and, if we can stand it, to remember when it was ours. If you do a survey of any room and ask who has ever fallen in love with the wrong person, what you'll likely meet is a gale of laughter, and then a sheepish show of hands, and then an uncomfortable silence. We've *all* fallen in love with the wrong person, and if we haven't, we will. This, too, is the way of human beings. And it doesn't matter how old we are, or how available we are; it just happens. Ask an adolescent. Middle school is all about falling for the wrong person, because everyone's out of your league. And all this drama may be great for the music industry—there would hardly be a song on the radio without it—but it's not so great for the one who falls.

It's Amnon's turn to fall now—to fall for the wrong person. And we might feel for him until we read the next string of verbs, which tell us how he handled it. *Amnon was so tormented that he made himself ill because of his sister Tamar, because she was a virgin, and it seemed impossible to Amnon to do anything to her*.

Amnon fell in love, but he didn't fall sick; he "made himself ill," which lets us know he's back in charge of his verbs. And what he chooses to do is to cultivate this illness, nourish it, feed it, like an impossible obsession. Why "impossible," by the way? Not because she's his sister. *Because she's a virgin*. There will be unmistakable physical evidence. David didn't have to consider the virginity issue with Bathsheba; she was married. But with Tamar, Amnon has to consider it; he can't *do anything to her*—not "with," by the way; "to."

As if she were an object he could pick up and put down at will. As if love, in the world according to Amnon, has no use for mutuality. It's just something he gets to *do* . . . to anyone he wants.

Amnon may not have had control over *falling in love*, but he did have control over *making himself ill* because of what he couldn't *do to her*—which is stomach-churning phrasing, at best, but also the chilling sound of a predator, sniffing the air. It leads us straight into a quick sidebar about adjectives—which, as we recall, are rare in Scripture. Tamar's adjective is "beautiful." Apparently this is why she caught Amnon's attention in the first place; the men in this royal family are good at the male gaze. Amnon's adjective is "haggard," which is also eye-catching, in its way, and no surprise for a person who's *making himself ill*. When you sit around stressed and obsessed all day, losing sleep and weight and the bloom in your cheeks, you're going to look haggard—and people will notice. They'll see the change in you and worry. They'll ask you what's wrong.

Jonadab, Amnon's friend and cousin, did exactly that: *"Son of the king, why are you so haggard morning after morning? Will you not tell me?"* Jonadab's concern would be a fine thing, except that Jonadab has an adjective, too: "crafty." *Jonadab was a very crafty man*, the text informs us. Run that adjective through your biblical echo chamber, and where does it lead? Straight to Genesis 3 and the serpent, who was more crafty than any of the other wild animals. And now we know all we need to know about Jonadab. The man is a snake.

Here's the first place in this story where things could have gone differently. Jonadab asks, and Amnon tells, and while *tell* is a good verb to choose when you fall in love with the wrong person, you have to be careful whom you tell. Tell the right person, and the urge to confide, to share, to bring into the light may lead to honest healing. Tell the wrong person, and a world of hurt follows. Amnon tells the wrong person. He tells the friend whose adjective is "crafty," not "wise," which means whatever Jonadab has to say about this situation is going to be as slippery and shrewd as he is. The ship could have turned around right here if Amnon had told the wise friend (who would have said something along the lines of "Oh, my goodness—I'm so sorry—and look, we're going to get through this together, because you know this can't happen, right?—*it cannot happen!*"). But Amnon didn't. He told Jonadab, whose advice is only as good as his adjective. And before we jump onto that condemn-the-crown-prince bandwagon again, let's take another pause to consider the script. How many of us have ever gotten bad advice from a friend? And how many of us have ever deliberately gone to the friend who we *knew* would give us bad advice, because it's what we wanted to hear?

Jonadab's advice is worse than we feared. *"Lie down on your bed and pretend to be ill, and when your father comes to see you, say to him, 'Let my sister Tamar come and give me something to eat, and prepare the food in my sight, so that I may see it and eat it from her hand.'"* It is a carefully crafted string of verbs, calculated to get Amnon what he wants: the girl in his room. That's the sort of friend Jonadab is. Tell him the truth, and he'll teach you how to pretend. Bring him on board, and he'll throw chum in the water.

Amnon had a moment when he might have steadied this pitching vessel, yet he chose to let it go—and bring on more predatory verbs. He fell in love with the wrong person, which was beyond his control. But he fed the beast, which was within his control. And pieces of that script, if we're brutally honest with ourselves, we recognize. Yes, we do.

It Could Have Gone Differently: Parents' Verbs

Amnon does as Jonadab schemes, and, sure enough, here comes King David to check on his firstborn. A crown prince can't sneeze without the press going nuts, as our British friends will confirm. Pretending to be ill, Amnon repeats Jonadab's words almost verbatim: *"Please let my sister Tamar come and make a couple of cakes in my sight, so that I may eat from her hand."*

This is the next place where things could have gone differently. David doesn't pick up on his son's slightly off-kilter request. Or he doesn't want to pick up on it. And parts of that script, we can understand. To acknowledge that there might be something wrong here—a half-brother wanting a private bedroom audience with his half-sister—is venturing into unthinkable territory, and, by definition, we don't gravitate toward the unthinkable, especially with our own children. It's why incest can be such a shock to parents, even when all the signs are there. Unthinkable. Unspeakable. And yet. And then.

But that precedent we spoke of, the one David unleashed, is roaming the palace grounds, and there are definite warning signs. Amnon is haggard: that raises concerns. He wants Tamar alone in his room: that raises eyebrows. It might even cross the line and go way out of bounds, even for a crown prince. Should David have noticed and been alarmed? Yes. No. Yes. All we have to go on are his verbs: *David sent home to Tamar, saying, "Go to your brother Amnon's house, and prepare food for him."* Two imperatives, delivered by messenger, and shortened to a few clipped commands, as if all that "in my sight" language were a little too much, and a little too close. Because what would David really have to do to think the unthinkable about his firstborn? He'd have to look at himself in an agonizingly clear mirror. And that would reveal all his terrible verbs from the previous chapters with Bathsheba, the ones Amnon has been studying and fantasizing about—and now, is asking his father to collude in. *Take. Pretend. Send. Come on, Dad; you know what I want.*

This is one of those huge moments in a parent's life, and David blows it. He won't step up. He won't take control of his son's out-of-control verbs. It could have gone differently. But then David would have had to do something even harder than confessing to the prophet Nathan. He would have had to turn his gaze on his own actions and admit how they've shaped his own children. And that takes the courage of a mighty king.

It Could Have Gone Differently: Bystanders' Verbs

When nighttime predators are loose and on the hunt within the walls of the palace, no one is safe. Everyone, from the king to the servants, will eventually come within range; everyone will be affected. And even the minor characters will have decisions to make about the verbs they use—decisions which could alter the course of events. Or keep them steamrolling along.

After David orders Tamar to Amnon's quarters, she goes, without comment: *So Tamar went to her brother Amnon's house, where he was lying down. She took dough, kneaded it, made cakes in his sight, and baked the cakes. Then she took the pan and set them out before him, but he refused to eat.* Note how many verbs it takes to make a couple of cakes; we assume she was there for a while. Note, too, that she has to perform each one of those verbs "in his sight": we assume *kneading* must have been particularly trying. He sits back and watches her, feasts his eyes, which is exactly what he wanted and what his friend and his father helped him orchestrate; it is the prelude, a form of visual pornography. She says not a word; she just finishes the task and sets the pan before him. But he refuses to eat. He has other verbs in mind.

To pull them off, he first has to clear the room—and this is the next place where things could have gone differently. *Amnon said, "Send out everyone from me." So everyone went out from him.* This is when the spotlight suddenly shifts to the bystanders, who, as it turns out, were also in the room, with front-row seats. Servants, most likely; his and hers. And even though something's going on here that everyone can smell and see, and perhaps has even seen coming, they all get up and leave; they leave her alone, with him. And what would have happened if they hadn't?

Yes, there's a serious power dynamic here: the prince has it, and the servants don't. Amnon gives the orders, and they must obey; when he *sends out*, they *go out*. If they don't, they lose their jobs—or their heads. It makes the situation very complicated, because they're at risk: no matter what they do, lives and livelihoods are at stake.

And who doesn't know what that's like? To look the other way, because someone told you it was your job? To leave the room, because someone instructed you, "You're not liable and you're not responsible for what happens here; just do your job over there." Feelings are supposed to be irrelevant, which is why we say inane things like "Sorry, ma'am, it's nothing personal—I'm just doing my job." But it's always personal when someone's at risk. It's personal for Tamar. So you have to ask yourself: Are the verbs that could happen to her less important than the verbs that could happen to me? And why has my job suddenly turned into fig leaves that can't cover any of us?

The bystanders' script is one we must seriously consider. We may not be servants of an ancient Near Eastern king in the Bronze Age whose lives will be hanging by a thread if we so much as cough in the crown prince's presence, but we know what it's like to be part of the crowd that's watching, witnessing, and choosing not to get involved as a tense scene unfolds. Choosing to hang back when the drama erupts. Choosing to remain silent when the violence is done. Choosing to protect our own verbs rather than those of a person we aren't, technically, responsible for—and ignoring her bruises and her black eye, too. It's none of our business. It's not our job.

If one bystander had taken control of a verb here—chosen *stay* or *shout* or *go for help*—things might have gone differently. They might have gone differently for an entire kingdom. And saved one family, in the process, and the woman they cast overboard.

Tamar's Verbs and the End of the Line

Tamar has some verbs of her own. She delivers what is probably the most rhetorically perfect argument in Scripture: the case against rape, start to finish, in seven irrefutable points.

1. No. I'm saying no.
2. You're my brother.
3. We don't do this in Israel. It's not who we are.
4. This act has an adjective: *vile.*
5. What would happen to me? I would have nowhere to go.
6. What would happen to you? You would be one of the scoundrels in Israel.

7. If it has to happen, if it's really about to happen, at least talk to Dad first—because we both know he won't withhold me from you.

It's an astounding speech, especially when contrasted with Bathsheba's silence in the previous two chapters. But it doesn't hold against Amnon's verbs, which are *would not listen* and *being stronger*. He was stronger, and so he forced her—because he could. He wanted and took—because he could. The precedent has struck another member of the family.

Tamar's final set of verbs is a breathtaking act of resistance in the wake of the crime. In a rage of loathing, Amnon calls his servant (painfully, within earshot) and orders him to *put this woman out* and *bolt* the door after her—as if the very sight of her, now, were abhorrent. Tamar responds by tearing her robe, putting ashes on her head, and taking to the corridors, *crying aloud* as she goes. It's a mourning script, but it's also a prophetic one; the prophets of Israel "cried aloud" in times of injustice. And she makes sure that everyone in the palace sees and hears, even though Amnon wouldn't. She *makes a scene*, one that any activist would respect. "Look at my wretchedness!" she might as well be crying. "Listen to me scream! I'll make sure your eyes are opened to what we've become in this palace—and the verbs we've set loose to devour us!"

There are more heart-wrenching stops to make in this text, places where it could have gone differently, but we'll mention just three more from the family circle. Tamar's brother, Absalom, advises her to *be quiet for now*—a script which bears an uncanny resemblance to the one women are still ordered to take, and still speaking up to expose. Tamar's father, King David, hears of "these things" and is angry, but *would not punish* his beloved firstborn son—a script which continues to play out in the sentencing of men convicted of assault. And then Absalom gets the last stop. He *speaks neither good nor bad* to his brother Amnon. We aren't sure whether he's biding his time to make a play for the throne or truly sickened by his brother's actions. But we do know there's nothing between these brothers now but hate.

And that's where the story ends: a terminus of ruins. We're left wondering what might have gone differently if the father had punished, or the younger son had spoken up; perhaps a measure of integrity could have been restored to the kingdom, with justice for Tamar. It would have required deeply painful speech and action, much harder than David's atonement for his sins of two chapters ago, because now we're talking about the atonement of an entire family. But it could have happened. And it didn't. And a few chapters later, these boys of David are dead on the set, and his beautiful daughter has disappeared.

God in the Imagining, God in the Speaking

Now that we've read and rehearsed just a small bit of this text and done our best to stay in the scene, what do we say? What do we do? Where is God in a story in which God's name is never mentioned?

It's our task, as a group in the repertory church, to say something. Not about how we feel, although we can discuss that. Not about ourselves, although we can share that, too. Our task is to say something about God, and even a text that never mentions the Holy Name is teeming with evidence about who this God is. So we listen to what is said as well as what isn't said, and we enter the verbs that are chosen as well as the ones that weren't, but could have been. That's especially important with a text of terror. If we couldn't imagine other possibilities than those written, we would crumple under the weight of despair. So God is in the imagining; that's rehearsal. And then it's time to speak.

Here's some of the amazing wisdom I've heard around the wide repertory church when I've read this text with groups in many places.

A Pentecostal pastor in Alabama said, "The place in the text that gets me is verse 7: *Then David sent home to Tamar, saying, 'Go to your brother Amnon's house, and prepare food for him.'* And the reason it gets me," she said, "is that I had a strong and wonderful father who loved me with all his heart. He would never have done this to me. He would never have put me in harm's way. He knew the horror in the world—as an African-American man in the South, he knew it well—and he protected me and raised me to know my own worth and strength. And what I know about God," said this pastor, "is that God is that kind of father: strong, courageous, sheltering, loving. So what I want to say is this: *If you don't have a father, or if your father is none of these things, God will fill that role for you. God will be the parent who lifts you up.*"

A Lutheran chaplain in a northern city said, "The place in the text that gets me is in verse 20: *'Be quiet for now'*—Absalom's words to Tamar. And the reason it gets me," he said, "is because a priest in our church was brought up on charges of sexual misconduct, and the women who accused him were handed this script. They were told, 'Be quiet for now. He is our priest.' We were more worried about our church than about these women. And what I know about God," said this chaplain, "is that God never sanctions silence as a fig-leaf cover-up. God is walking in the woods around every person who told those women to be quiet, and God is calling, 'Where are you?' So what I want to say is this: *You can't ever tell someone to be quiet if you have a stake in the quiet. That's as good as a cover-up, and we as a church have got to repent.*"

A young Baptist pastor from Texas said, "The place in the text that gets me is in verse 22: *Absalom spoke to Amnon neither good nor bad.* And the reason it gets me," he said, "is because I look around our church, and I see how some of us never say a word about what is going on. We're sick of the divisions and the fighting among ourselves, or we don't want to get involved, or we're looking out for our own careers and know there are consequences to speaking either good or bad. So we don't say anything. We choose a script of silently biding our time: Absalom's script. And what I know about God," said this pastor, "is that God calls us to speak truth—not 'neither good nor bad,' or what will play out best for us and our own advancement. So what I want to say is this: *We are not the church of Absalom. We are the church of Jesus Christ.*"

A pastor in a Scandinavian country said, "The place in the text that gets me is in verse 14: *being stronger than she was, Amnon forced her and lay with her.* And the reason it gets me," he said, "is that a lot of men in my country don't know the script for being a man anymore. We don't know how to handle the idea that we are often physically stronger than the women we live and work with, but that this does not entitle us to use that strength against them, just because we can. And so we're trying to be sensitive and gentle and strong in other ways, but what do we do with our rage, when it comes? What I know about God," said this pastor, "is that God shows us what real strength is: to break the chains of the oppressed, and to set the captives free, and to love and serve and fear the Lord as Jesus did. So what I want to say is this: *God calls each of us to understand our own strength, and how it can be used for good and for ill—and then God calls us to be strong in the Lord, not in our own power.*"

A young Nazarene woman in Tennessee said, "The place in the text that gets me is in verse 19, when Tamar puts ashes on her head and tears her clothes and goes away crying aloud. And the reason it gets me," she said, "is that women are really taught not to make a scene. We're supposed to stuff our pain and our hurt, even when we've been violated, and never show it in public. Never show our wounds or cry aloud in a way that will disturb the peace. It's a terrible script, with devastating results. And what I know about God," said this woman, "is that God calls prophets to cry out to the people. 'Crying out' is a prophetic verb, and there is a time for it. So what I want to say is this: *If you are Tamar, whether you are a man or a woman, you can tell us and show us what has happened to you, and we as a community can take it; we will take it and bear it. Because if we don't, our church and our nation will fall apart as surely as King David's did.*"

The Blessing and Charge of a Word to Speak

The hardest part about reading hard texts is opening them—and staying in the scene. But with the repertory church, the task is shared and lightened. These are not nouns we have to carry until they break our backs and hearts. These are not verbs we have to suffer alone or deny. We can claim the strength of standing together. We can claim the courage of planting our feet. And we can claim the freedom of imagining new endings—where things might go differently, so life can flourish.

Avoiding these texts is like letting the hunter continue to stalk. Worse, it's letting that night prowler have the last word. But reading and rehearsing a text, any text—and a text of terror, most of all—defies a terminus of ruins. It defuses the power that wants only to brutalize. It opens the way to blessing and truth. Now we're free to walk straight into any story, farther than we'd ever dared, because we know we *can* come back and say something true. We know it's part of our calling. And we know there's nothing that can separate us from the love of God in Christ Jesus, not even the scripts in this text.

Where have you seen God moving in the midst of our reading? Perhaps you've been given a word to speak, a word that will bless and be a blessing. A word that may breathe hope into ruins. A word that may summon grace to rise, and a woman who walks the corridors of the sea.

CHAPTER 9

Changing One Verb

Reading and Rehearsing Exodus 3

Some stories in Scripture are so familiar and so well loved that I think of them as "greatest hits": year after year we just keep playing them. Moses at the burning bush is a story like that. It shows up in Sunday school and at the box office, in logo designs and on church banners. It's also a classic way for a person to describe a "call" experience: the moment we feel God is *addressing* and *sending* us somewhere we never expected to go, for work or ministry we never believed we could do. Burning bush moments are watershed moments. They mark a turning point, like the day you met your spouse. And just like that story, a burning bush story is one we'll probably tell many times over the years—maybe using before-and-after language to mark the shift (". . . once I was like Moses, just tending sheep and minding my own business, and the next thing I knew, I was on my way to Pharaoh. . . .").

But the older we get, the farther away a burning bush moment can seem. Life happens, the work continues, and this story from Exodus 3 feels like something that happened long ago and far away. It's a script we played once, back at the beginning, and then tucked away in a memory book for safekeeping. When we hear the story now, we listen from the middle of wherever we happen to be, in life and in work–from the *middle* of ministry–and when we tell it, we sound like old-timers around the campfire. But it doesn't seem to belong to us anymore, the way it once did.

But what if Exodus 3 isn't just about beginnings? What if this is a script we get to play more than once over the course of a life? What if it keeps coming up, like a greatest hits song? One day, when I was in a middling frame of mind, I asked myself–and some others who were in-the-middle sorts–to listen to Exodus 3 again. And not as if we were trying to hear it the way we once did, back at the beginning, but as if we were always meant to hear it from *exactly where we are,* in the middle of our own stories–as if that, too, were Moses's holy ground. What is possible to hear from the middle that we might have missed at the beginning? And then we wondered what might happen if we changed our verbs, like Moses does, in the very first verse.

Sometimes, all it takes to re-enter a script is to follow the text's lead: change up one verb. See where it leads. And loosen those sandals. Let's take another look at the passage.

EXODUS 3:1–14

> 1 Moses was keeping the flock of his father-in-law Jethro, the
> priest of Midian; he led his flock beyond the wilderness, and
> came to Horeb, the mountain of God. 2 There the angel of the
> LORD appeared to Moses in a flame of fire out of a bush; he
> looked, and the bush was blazing, yet it was not consumed.
> 3 Then Moses said, "I must turn aside and look at this great
> sight, and see why the bush is not burned up." 4 When the
> LORD saw that Moses had turned aside to see, God called to

> him out of the bush, "Moses, Moses!" And he said, "Here I am." 5 Then the LORD said, "Come no closer! Remove the sandals from your feet, for the place on which you are standing is holy ground." 6 God said further, "I am the God of your father, the God of Abraham, the God of Isaac, and the God of Jacob." And Moses hid his face, for he was afraid to look at God. 7 Then the LORD said, "I have observed the misery of my people who are in Egypt; I have heard their cry on account of their taskmasters. Indeed, I know their sufferings, 8 and I have come down to deliver them from the Egyptians, and to bring them up out of that land to a good and broad land, a land flowing with milk and honey, to the country of the Canaanites, the Hittites, the Amorites, the Perizzites, the Hivites, and the Jebusites. 9 The cry of the Israelites has now come to me; I have also seen how the Egyptians oppress them. 10 So come, I will send you to Pharaoh to bring my people, the Israelites, out of Egypt." 11 But Moses said to God, "Who am I that I should go to Pharaoh, and bring the Israelites out of Egypt?" 12 God said, "I will be with you; and this shall be the sign for you that it is I who sent you: when you have brought the people out of Egypt, you shall worship God on this mountain." 13 But Moses said to God, "If I come to the Israelites and say to them, 'The God of your ancestors has sent me to you,' and they ask me, 'What is his name?' what shall I say to them?" 14 God said to Moses, "I AM WHO I AM." God said further, "Thus you shall say to the Israelites, 'I AM has sent me to you.'"

As a teacher, one thing I've learned over the years is that new students look very different in October than they do in September. It takes about a month for them to begin to feel at home and lose that deer-in-headlights look so many of them had at the beginning of term. I remember having that look myself, and maybe you do, too—that maybe this was all a mistake, and seminary (in my case) was a really bad idea, and when God called us to *"Go!"*, God didn't mean *here*. Remember that? The feeling that you've somehow ended up in the completely wrong place? Everybody feels that at some point or another. Everybody wonders if they're doing what God called them to do. We even wonder, these days, if the church is doing what God called it to do, or whether we somehow read the wrong shrubbery.

The call of Moses in Exodus 3 is a very comforting story if you're in a moment of second-guessing your own call. The dialogue that's already playing in your head is right there: *Who am I, that I should go? If I go, what do I say? If I say it, what if they don't believe me?—since I'm no good at talking. So please—send someone else!* Moses, who was The Great Staller before he was The Great Deliverer, tried every delaying tactic he could think of before he ran out of excuses; he wrote the script on evasion, which is reassuring when you need one. And we all do, at some point. We all say his lines. That's why this is such a good text for beginnings, when we're fearfully unsure, and why so many chapel talks at the start of the school year feature Moses in Exodus 3.

And then there are other seasons, like middles. When you're not at the beginning anymore, but *in the middle* of your call, your work, your ministry, your marriage; when you're mid-career, mid-life, mid-fall, mid-semester, in a calling and a church that may be past their expiration dates. When you're a middler, what does Exodus 3 have to say to *you*? Is it still a good text for a middle season? And if it is—which I suspect is true—what can we hear in it that we might have missed at the beginning?

The Middle of Midian

There comes a day when, as far as you can tell, your moment at the burning bush was a while ago. God called, you answered, you took one step forward, then two, and now, you're down the road, apparently doing what God called you to do. Apparently, this is Egypt. And you're leading people out—right? Out of oppression into freedom. Out of enslavement to a gender-privileged, hetero-privileged, economically stratified, consumer-addicted empire of white supremacy—since Pharaoh takes many forms. We're in the middle of that work, that ministry. Leading various flocks. And it's good work, holy work; it's God's work, we think. It's just got a lot of daily-ness to it, and repetition, and here-we-go-again routine that doesn't always feel like the road to liberation. Not the way we pictured it at the beginning.

Moses was in a season of middles in Exodus 3. He was in the middle of Midian, which is just what it sounds like. And I bet he thought there weren't a lot of seasons of beginnings left out there for him. Statistically speaking, given his age. Somewhere else, long ago, there had been excitement and drama, and he had even been Pharaoh's most-wanted man for murder—of Egyptian law enforcement, no less—but that was years ago, when he was young. Now he was settled in Midian. He had the family, he had the job—working for his father-in-law, actually: the flocks and herds business. Moses was in charge of keeping a flock. But he didn't own it; Jethro did—Jethro was an important man—so Moses worked for him and never had his own shop. And maybe he was fine with that. Maybe an associate position with Jethro exactly suited his gifts and temperament and time of life. But I do notice that the text is very clear. Right off the top, in verse 1, it emphasizes that *Moses was keeping the flock of his father-in-law, Jethro, the priest of Midian*—not his own flock. As if Moses hadn't yet risen in the local leadership ranks, or had risen all he was going to rise: middle management, mid-size business, mid-Sinai, rural setting. The middle of Midian.

That's the context when this chapter opens: Moses is keeping a flock in the middle of ministry, in the middle of Midian; there's nothing flashy, nothing noteworthy; even the verb, "keeping," is a kind of maintenance verb. Like getting up on an ordinary Wednesday: breakfast, dishes, morning commute, office; keeping appointments, keeping to the schedule and the budget, keeping up with trends and the to-do list, keeping an eye on the kids and social media, keeping the peace at the committee meeting and the dinner table and the session and the board, because those are the responsible things to do, when you're in the middle of work and ministry in a tired little place in Midian: you just . . . *keep* . . . things; you keep them going. Exodus 3 starts right there, in a middle season, in ordinary time: Moses was keeping the flock.

And then there's a little shift, a slight movement. The verb changes, and the place changes, and suddenly we're not in ordinary time anymore. Verse 1 again: "Moses was keeping the flock of his father-in-law, Jethro, the priest of Midian; he led his flock beyond the wilderness, and came to Horeb, the mountain of God."

Beyond the Wilderness

Actually, there are two little shifts. The first is the verb: *He led his flock beyond the wilderness*. No more maintenance; no more keeping. Moses got up and *led* that flock, which shepherds do from time to time. They *lead* when the flock needs to *go* places: green pastures, still waters; *in* paths of righteousness, *through* the wilderness—all the obvious locations for happy flocks. But Moses didn't lead his flock to any of those.

Then there's the second shift. He led it *beyond the wilderness.* Which is an odd expression, and practice, when you think about it: Why would you ever want to lead a flock there? Other translations say Moses took it to the back of the desert, or to its edge or its inner parts, or (my favorite) to the far side. To my ear, these versions are all saying a similar thing, which is *Yes, this place is remote and hard to reach, but it's more than that: it's beyond the wilderness we know. It's pushing the limits of wild.* And it's pushing *us*: whatever wilderness means to you, *this* place is one step beyond that.

Moses was keeping the flock in Midian, and he led it beyond the wilderness. And then, *then* he came to the mountain of God.

I don't know if Moses meant to do any of this. I don't know if he planned it or stumbled into it; I can imagine a lot of different scenarios. Maybe he got up that morning and decided, "Enough of Midian. Let's go to the mountain of God!" Like when some men turn fifty and think, "Kilimanjaro: it's now or never!" And then they book a spot with a trekking company and fly to Tanzania. It could have been a midlife thing for Moses—part pilgrimage, part adventure, part Buzz Lightyear: "To the wilderness and beyond!" Or maybe the whole thing was a glorious accident. Maybe Moses wasn't looking for Horeb at all; maybe he was looking for better grazing land for his flock, or a stream that wasn't dried up, and one path led to another, and there they were: beyond the wilderness, with—holy cow—the mountain of God right in front of them.

However it happened, the text is clear about one thing. Moses started in Midian and came to Horeb, *when he led his flock beyond where they usually went.* They had to leave what they knew and push past where they'd been. And then they were in a position to see it: the mountain of God, where a bush was burning and, for all we know, had been burning there for years, waiting for Moses to come.

There the angel of the LORD *appeared to Moses in a flame of fire out of a bush.* If you're in a season of middles, this is such perfect way for an angel to show up. Not in Midian, while you're sitting on the couch watching Netflix or the Falcons, which an angel of the Lord could certainly choose to do, but that doesn't seem to happen much. If you're in a middle season, like Moses, maybe you have to get off the couch to see your angel of the Lord. Maybe you need a push to go somewhere new and really look. So a burning bush on the mountain of God that's beyond the wilderness yet still quite close to Midian is perfect. It's not so far from home that you can't get there; you can. It's not so off-grid that you won't find it; you will. And it's just understated enough to require some skill and maturity to see: a little bush in flames—blazing, yet not consumed. Moses had to turn aside to look. But he also had to *get* there to look. Get his body and his flock to the mountain of God. In two small shifts. Where the angel of the Lord was planning to appear in a display tailor-made for him.

Moses said, "I must turn aside and look at this great sight, and see why the bush is not burned up." And this, you could argue, is where the Exodus really begins. The verse is a road map for deep engagement: *turn aside, look, find out why.* Because this bush isn't scenery you happen to notice from your car as you speed past at sixty miles per hour. You've got to stop the car and park and get out. *Turn aside.* Take a detour. Get distracted. Interrupt. This is a great sight, or an awful sight, or a disturbing, confounding, heartbreaking sight, and it deserves our full attention. Turn aside, and then *look*. Really look. Put down the iPhone. Crouch down, climb up, get close, as close as you can, and look. This is an art the world has mostly forgotten but which the work of ministry, in all its forms, honors: *to look at what no one else wants to see*. It's an act of reverence. It's an act of resistance. It's an act of unbelievable courage and love. Turn aside and look. And then ask the question that Pharaoh doesn't want you to ask. Why? Why is this bush burning yet not consumed? Why is God showing up in a desert, in Midian, with news about slavery in Egypt? And why on earth would God think you could make any difference in dismantling that, when the only verb sequence you've perfected is to *keep things going*?

Moses said, "I must turn aside and look at this great sight, and see why the bush is not consumed." And as soon as he did that, he was on holy ground. He was ready to be addressed by The One Who Is Who That One Is. And he was ready to be sent. Or almost ready. After five pretty lame attempts to get out of it, which, I must say, sound awfully familiar.

Leaving Midian

Moses in Midian. I don't think that's a script we play only once in our lives. I don't think God's call to us is a one-time, watershed moment that launches us into our particular line of work and ministry fully formed, wonderfully made. I might have, once. Before I got to Midian and realized how seductive maintenance can be. It can really get ahold of you, the pressure to keep things going. And then keep them just the same. Keep the organization or the church or the job just the same. Without asking why. Without turning aside to see anything but the next thing on your calendar.

But from the middle of ministry, I wonder if this text is meant to be played more than once. Maybe rather than asking each other about our call stories—those burning-bush moments from long ago and far away—we should start asking each other about the last time we left Midian. And if it seems like we've been there for a while, keeping up with everything that working for Jethro requires, maybe that's a signal: time to change up the verb. Change up the location. And not just ourselves—the flock, too. Figure out what *behind the wilderness* looks like, for all of us, and just plunge in; lead 'em straight to it, and beyond it. Apparently, that's the way to the mountain of God, and to a burning bush that's been waiting for us, all along.

I'm not underestimating how difficult this is. Leaving Midian entails asking a lot of hard questions, and each one leads us closer to Pharaoh's palace and the slave quarters behind it. Each one takes us deeper into the systems of oppression that Egypt employs to feed its appetites. Every "Why?" leads to another "Why?," and before we know it, we're taking a good, hard look at our complicity in those systems, and how "keeping things going" was what Pharaoh wanted us to do all along. "Keeping things going" in Midian is what props up slavery in Egypt. And it always will—until we break the cycle of maintenance.

If we thought we were too mediocre-in-the-middle for this journey back to Egypt, we wouldn't be the first. But God isn't sending us to relive old mistakes, the times we thought justice was something we could take into our own hands, in anger and violence, and later bury in the sand. God is sending us to be witnesses to *God's* justice–witnesses and partners. Because this is the promise of that one changed-up verb: Midian is not our home. Maintenance is not our work. Our call is to find a path to the mountain of God, over and over, so that even in the middle of wherever we are, we can be interrupted by a great sight and another sending.

I think there's a burning bush that has your name on it. Turn aside, and look.

CHAPTER 10

A Truth for the World

Reading and Rehearsing the Book of Esther

In the spring, I teach a class called "Back to the Text." The idea is simple. I pick a book of Scripture, the students read all the scholarly literature about it that they can digest, and once a week we gather to read through the entire book together. At the end of the semester we perform it for the seminary community. We've done the Gospel of Mark, large portions of Luke and John, the books of Exodus and Esther and Daniel and Job, and 1 Timothy.

"Back to the Text" has become one of my favorite classes, which is a little strange because there isn't any preaching in the course, and, officially, that's what I teach. But I love this class because of what it does to us as a reading community. By the end of the semester, when we perform the Scripture, we're fiercely in love with it; it's inside us, and we carry it everywhere. We don't memorize it—that isn't the goal—but we make interpretive choices together about how we want to stage it, because we've read it so many times by then.

The first eight weeks of the class, we read the verbs and rehearse the text using all the material from Chapters 3 and 4 of this book. We read it sitting around a table, verse by verse; we read it while improvising the action; we read it with different subtexts; we read it imagining we're an underground community of persecuted believers who could be killed for possessing the book itself. We read it while roaming around campus, and we read it with women taking men's parts and men taking women's parts. We dress up, we dress down, we do it with choreography, we do it in drag. Every reading shows us something new. And over the semester, we learn how rich it is to read Scripture as a group in the repertory church—with the freedom to rehearse it, and experiment with it, and fall in love with it.

Rehearsal Gets Real

One spring, as my class and I were working on the book of Esther, the festival of Purim took place in the first week of March, midway through the semester. It seemed logical that we would attend services, since Purim is the festival that celebrates Esther. I called around to several synagogues and asked if we might visit. A nearby congregation of the United Synagogue of Conservative Judaism was especially friendly on the phone, so off we went on a Wednesday night: a wide-eyed group of mostly young, mostly Southern seminarians, all denominations, all races and backgrounds, all of whom had studied biblical Hebrew—but most of whom had never been to a synagogue. We kind of stood out. But you'd never have known it, given the ease with which the congregation received us—as though Protestant seminarians who like to read Esther showed up to worship with them every week. The rabbis welcomed us warmly, introduced us around, and told us to make ourselves at home. We joined a potluck dinner in progress—the children were having a costume parade, the youth group was selling boxes of macaroni and cheese for noisemakers—and just as the sun went down, we all filed into the sanctuary for worship.

So picture this. Up front was the rabbi in his Yankees baseball cap, pouring shots as well as little glasses of margaritas and mojitos, while he simultaneously chanted the scroll in Hebrew. To the right of him was the associate rabbi, resplendent in a costume of silk veils, running a live Twitter feed on a huge screen (a first, for this congregation); she invited all present to chime in with their cell phones, which they did when they weren't encouraging their children to make more noise with the macaroni boxes. When four members stood up to take their turns reading and chanting the scroll in Hebrew, a woman behind us whispered that they had been studying with the rabbis for months in preparation, because the melodies used to chant the book of Esther are especially intricate and hard to learn. Then the story our class knew so well unfolded, in Hebrew, and as it did, the congregation went wild. We sang, we stomped, we twittered; we drank and yelled whenever Haman's name was mentioned; we made jokes about the rabbi on the twitter feed, and he roared with laughter. Children ran up and down the aisles, teenagers texted, parents made a second trip to the drinks table, and after an hour of this, we all trooped out and ate hamantaschen, the traditional Purim cookies. By the time we left, the entire congregation was waving good-bye and inviting us to come back anytime; we would always be welcome, especially a group such as ours, with such reverence for Scripture.

Picture this, too. Out in the parking lot, after the service, our class was speechless as we fell into cars for the trip home. Sure, we'd been reading and rehearsing the book of Esther every week. But this was real. This was a real congregation, drinking real margaritas during real worship, and the rabbi was working the blenders and reading the text in Hebrew while wearing a Yankees hat in Atlanta, and no one was acting like there was anything unusual about this—in fact, they all looked completely calm, as if breaking every single rule they usually have about worship wasn't freaking them out, not in the slightest. Next week they'd be back to normal, with no margaritas or baseball caps or macaroni boxes or texting or twittering or jokes about the rabbi in their sanctuary—until Purim came around again.

It was a pivotal moment for our class. We knew the book of Esther is about parody and reversal. We just didn't know what it would be to enact that with a congregation. To push the limits, for one night, of what's acceptable. To make fun of the rabbi and ourselves. To do irreverent things in the sanctuary. And not just for the heck of it, because it's a class, and we can make exceptions. *This* pushing of the limits is what we do when we read a story about a genocide that almost happened, but didn't. *This* pushing of the limits is what we do when we read the book of Esther, the story of a Jewish woman who becomes Queen of Persia, hides who she is, and finally breaks her vow of silence in order to save her people. Her very name means "I am hiding." Esther pushes the limits of every limit that's possible to push, and stages a coming-out party for the king in order to tell him that she's a Jew. And if he goes through with his edict to kill all the Jews in Persia, he'll have to kill her, too.

My students knew all this. But rehearsing the book of Esther with that congregation tossed them into the deep end of the pool after a lot of practicing their strokes in the air, poolside. Now that they had experienced the truth of parody, they started to ask new questions. Why are issues of identity so often at the root of acts of violence? Does *hiding who we are* allow or perpetuate violence against others? Is claiming who we are, and living that out before God, a truth for the world that can save the world? And why is it so necessary to return to these questions every year and rehearse them in worship, in one big, boisterous festival? Does pushing against the sacred help us to remember what *is* sacred?

I can tell you that our conversation got a lot more interesting after our visit to the synagogue. Our weekly readings weren't just play for the sake of play. Now it was play for the sake of justice. It mattered. Real issues, real lives, were at stake. We were making connections between who we were, our constructed identities, and the acts of violence all around us. We were thinking about the power of coming out, in whatever form that verb takes for each of us, and how it overturns the power of this world.

Epiphany—and Some Road Markers

Do you want to know the *why* of all this reading the verbs and rehearsing the text, this script in Scripture, with the repertory church? It is this. Out of the blue, in the middle of a margarita in worship, we got it: this isn't about me, or us, or our wildly experimental group with its brilliantly inventive interpretations. *This is about justice for the oppressed. This is about liberation for the captives. This is about the realm of God breaking its way in, and we just saw a flash of its truth right here. So let's follow it, because Lord, we want to be in that number when the redeemed saints go marching in.*

I wish I could tell you how that moment of epiphany happens. I can't. But I can tell you it's why my students and I read verbs like crazy people, why we rehearse Scripture as a group, why we jump in and hang on to the text and one another. We're waiting for it—the moment when we see something true. We want to speak a truth for the world.

I can also tell you there are there some road markers to watch for, ways to name aspects of that epiphany as it's unfolding. *How* it happens may be a mystery, but what it looks and feels like along the way is very evident in the moment.

Four road markers in particular are helpful to watch for. They come from the field of performance studies by way of Richard Schechner, one of the field's founding scholars. Schechner has written that every performance, no matter what it is, has four aspects. For the repertory church, I think of them as road markers for our reading of Scripture, and you'll notice that each makes an appearance in Chapter 4.

The first road marker shows that performance (which includes our reading of Scripture) is ***subjunctive.*** It deals in the "as if" tense, which lets us ask questions. What would happen if we tried this, or did that, or rehearsed the text *as if* we were teenagers, or soldiers, or girls in Afghanistan, or someone living with a terminal illness? What would happen if we read the book of Esther with a real congregation in worship? As we read, the subjunctive is the first road marker to look for. It allows us to rehearse different possibilities in freedom, yet with precision. In the "Back to the Text" class, this is what we do each week: change one variable and see what transpires.

The second road marker signals that performance is ***liminal.*** It plays at the edges, it works the angles, it pushes the limits of what's possible. It takes us past the margins of what might be acceptable, or thinkable, or believable, or possible. So consider our class trip to the synagogue: when we walked into the sanctuary and the rabbi offered us *drinks*, some of my students had to really check themselves. A few were teetotaling Baptists; they didn't drink alcohol, and the "in worship" part of this drinking equation was blowing their minds. They had to be very stern with themselves and remember the liminal nature of performance so they could physically stay put and not flee the scene. It was a big move for them, and I was proud they did it. But they couldn't have if they hadn't known to look for that liminal road marker. It oriented them so they had space to wonder: What is truly profane in this world? Margaritas in worship? Or genocide we ignore and do nothing to stop?

The third road marker indicates that performance is ***duplicitous.*** What's happening on the stage isn't "the real world" as we know it—but it's more *real* than the reality we so often live. It has the ring of truth. It resonates deep down; it opens doors we thought we'd locked tight. It shows us who we really are, or could be. Not all the time, not every moment, but in flashes, in fragments. Often enough for us to need reminding that what's taking place on the stage isn't happening in real life and real time, no matter how real it looks. When a character in a play murders another character, for example, we know the actors are using fake swords—or at least we hope they are. We expect that what's happening on that stage is theater. So why does it seem to hold more truth than our everyday lives do? Why does dressing up in costumes for Purim show us more about who we really are, behind the invisible masks we wear every day? Because performance shows us a duplicitous sort of truth: not real, yet more real than the world we know, the reality we live in.

The fourth and last road marker warns that performance is ***dangerous.*** Real lives are affected. Real change happens, sometimes in ways that are totally disruptive. A lighter version of this is the tendency for leading actors who play opposite one another to actually fall in love, offstage, which happens a lot—and seems romantic, unless you're no longer a teenager, and what you've fallen in love with is a mirage. A heavier version of this is what happens in the book of Esther, when Esther weighs the agonizing risks of revealing her Jewish identity or continuing to hide it. Coming out is dangerous for her; she could be killed. *Not* coming out is dangerous for her people; millions of them *will* be killed. So she conceives a performance before the king whose outcome she can't predict; she can only hope that he'll see and hear and stop the violence. And it works. But, going in, she doesn't know that. Performance can be dangerous for us, and it can have dangerous consequences for a people, a system, or a world as we know it.

These four road markers may not be the first thing you want to share with a group that's gathering to read Scripture together ("Welcome to what is sure to be, for all of us, a thrilling experience of the subjunctive, the liminal, the duplicitous, and the dangerous!"). You might find your numbers have dropped substantially the next week as people run for cover—which is why I've couched those markers in friendlier language in Chapter 4 ("Reading in Wolf Suits" counts as friendlier verbiage).

On the other hand, groups that have read and rehearsed Scripture together for any length of time have passed these road markers often. And they recognize them. They know when their group is in subjunctive territory—all those forks in the road to choose from—and they know that bumpy, uneven ground means they've crossed into a liminal space. They expect to see flashes of (duplicitous) insight on the horizon—or was it in the rearview mirror?—and they've spent enough nights in the wilderness to know that the journey is dangerous. Pharaoh's chariots are out there. So is a path to cross over. A group that gathers to read and rehearse Scripture can light that path with torches, and then others can cross over, too.

The Rehearsing Life

So, once more: Why do we do all this? Why make of Scripture such a *big production* where we read and rehearse, stay in the scene, block the action, change the verbs, switch roles, ask new questions, push the limits, fail gloriously, change our minds, and cross over—in real time and space?

Because these are the very scripts that will redeem all sinners and saints, and the earth we share. They are ours to read and play. And the Word is shimmering on every page.

Out of the blue, it hits us: *we've seen something true.*

So let's come back and tell it. And then live it, together.

Five More Tools for Rehearsing Scripture

APPENDIX 1

Gathering

A Group Process for Reading the Verbs

This is the process I use for reading the verbs in groups—as a repertory church. You and those reading with you might take it as a starting point and adapt as needed.

1. *Choose a Scripture passage (10–20 verses or so).* This is helpful to do ahead of time. The group can decide together what sort of biblical texts it's interested in reading (stories from Genesis? the parables of Jesus? an entire book? passages related to a theme?), or agree to take turns choosing the texts you'll read together. If you're part of a faith community that gathers for worship, you might start a practice of reading the texts that will be included in worship for the coming week.

2. *For each person, print out a copy in large type.* Some of us feel squeamish about marking up our Bibles. With copies, everyone has the freedom to underline, circle, scribble, and punctuate (or puncture) as much as they want. A printed copy for each person also gives everyone the same translation to work

through. Group members can still bring their own Bibles for reference or comparison, in whatever translations or languages are closest to them. (The differences in those translations are often thought-provoking!)

3. *Designate a convener for the day.* This person will keep the group moving through the process as it reads verse by verse. For the hour or so that your group is gathered, the convener also keeps time, calls breaks, and makes sure everyone is getting a chance to speak.

4. *Read the entire passage out loud, all the way through.* The convener invites the group to do this after they've gathered in a circle. Go around the circle, allowing each person the option to read one verse aloud (it's always fine to pass), until the group has read the whole passage. A microphone can be helpful if volume is a concern; no one should have to strain to be heard.

5. *Stop and take a moment.* At the end of the passage, the convener invites the group to pause and get its bearings before launching straight into conversation. Reading Scripture aloud does things to people; they'll need a moment to notice that. The convener might ask the group to take a few deep breaths, or to turn to those near them to offer a kind word or a greeting (such as "Peace be with you"). It's a way for the group to begin to pay attention to exactly what's happening as they read.

6. *Go back to the beginning and read one verse at a time, focusing on the verbs.* Picking up where you left off, the convener invites the next person in the circle to read aloud the first verse of the

passage. Then stop to name the verbs as a group. Take a few moments to talk about them. The convener can lead this discussion by prompting the group with questions from Chapter 3, or you may find the group doesn't need any prompting; everyone might jump right in. When you're ready, go on to the next verse, inviting the next person in the circle to read it aloud. Continue in this way, slowly, until you get to the end of the passage.

APPENDIX 2

Numbering

Nouns, Verbs, Adjectives, and Ratios

This is an exercise I do with a group the first time it meets so we can see the nouns-to-verbs-to-adjectives ratio at work. (The number of nouns and verbs are roughly equivalent; the number of adjectives are a fraction of that.) It makes the point, works as a good icebreaker, and gives everyone a refresher course in grammar, since many of us are years out from elementary school and have to be reminded about what nouns, verbs, and adjectives actually *are*.

Here's an easy way to facilitate this. Have your group pass around copies of the Scripture text and then divide itself into three sections. Everyone in the first section counts all the <u>nouns</u> in the passage: persons, places, things, ideas. (Don't let the pronouns hog more than their share, or they'll skew the count; each pronoun only gets one turn per sentence.) Everyone in the second section counts the <u>verbs</u>: action words. Everyone in the third section counts the <u>adjectives</u>: words that describe nouns. Take a few minutes for everyone to do the count quietly, on their own, and then another minute so they can compare their results with others in the same section. Then have each of the three sections—nouns first, verbs second, adjectives third—share its numbers with the whole group.

Most of the time, the numbers will speak for themselves, as long as the Noun People haven't lost their heads completely with the pronouns and tripled their numbers. You'll also find that the adjectives really do round out to about 10 percent of the noun-and-verb number. There are exceptions, of course. Head over to 1 Corinthians 13, where Paul assures us that love is *patient* and *kind*, and not *envious* or *boastful* or *arrogant* or *rude*, and you'll find yourself with a big stack of adjectives fairly quickly.

One important caveat: the results are meant to be illustrative, not definitive or conclusive. This means that when you do this exercise, you may not want to call in The Society of English Majors (or your language equivalent) to monitor the count for you, as it could lead to loud and tiresome debates about fussier parts of speech. The point is that you're looking for a general, in-the-ballpark sort of count here, to show that verbs and nouns are evenly represented in Scripture. If you're worried that some in your group may be too exacting with the numbers, enlist the help of a few nine-year-olds. They're learning about grammar in school, have an excellent grasp of the subject, and will be more than happy to keep the adults in a repertory church group in line.

To illustrate, here's how I counted the nouns, verbs, and adjectives in the Genesis 3 passage. (Spoiler alert: My count was forty-seven nouns, forty-six verbs, and seven adjectives. The ratio holds.)

GENESIS 3: NOUNS

1 Now the serpent was more crafty than any other wild animal that the LORD God had made. He said to the woman,

> "Did God say, 'You shall not eat from any tree in the gar-
> den'?" 2 The woman said to the serpent, "We may eat of the
> fruit of the trees in the garden; 3 but God said, 'You shall not
> eat of the fruit of the tree that is in the middle of the garden,
> nor shall you touch it, or you shall die.'" 4 But the serpent
> said to the woman, "You will not die; 5 for God knows that
> when you eat of it your eyes will be opened, and you will
> be like God, knowing good and evil." 6 So when the woman
> saw that the tree was good for food, and that it was a delight
> to the eyes, and that the tree was to be desired to make one
> wise, she took of its fruit and ate; and she also gave some to
> her husband, who was with her, and he ate.
>
> 7 Then the eyes of both were opened, and they knew
> that they were naked; and they sewed fig leaves together
> and made loincloths for themselves. 8 They heard the sound
> of the LORD God walking in the garden at the time of the
> evening breeze, and the man and his wife hid themselves
> from the presence of the LORD God among the trees of the
> garden. 9 But the LORD God called to the man, and said to
> him, "Where are you?" 10 He said, "I heard the sound of you
> in the garden, and I was afraid, because I was naked; and I
> hid myself."

My count is forty-seven nouns. You'll notice that if a noun or pronoun occurred repeatedly in a sentence, I only counted it once. You'll also notice that I counted as a single word any phrase joined together by the word "of," such as "fruit of the trees" and "sound of the evening breeze." You might do it differently, and that's fine.

GENESIS 3: VERBS

1 Now the serpent was more crafty than any other wild animal that the LORD God had made. He said to the woman, "Did God say, 'You shall not eat from any tree in the garden'?" 2 The woman said to the serpent, "We may eat of the fruit of the trees in the garden; 3 but God said, 'You shall not eat of the fruit of the tree that is in the middle of the garden, nor shall you touch it, or you shall die.'" 4 But the serpent said to the woman, "You will not die; 5 for God knows that when you eat of it your eyes will be opened, and you will be like God, knowing good and evil." 6 So when the woman saw that the tree was good for food, and that it was a delight to the eyes, and that the tree was to be desired to make one wise, she took of its fruit and ate; and she also gave some to her husband, who was with her, and he ate.

7 Then the eyes of both were opened, and they knew that they were naked; and they sewed fig leaves together and made loincloths for themselves. 8 They heard the sound of the LORD God walking in the garden at the time of the evening breeze, and the man and his wife hid themselves from the presence of the LORD God among the trees of the garden. 9 But the LORD God called to the man, and said to him, "Where are you?" 10 He said, "I heard the sound of you in the garden, and I was afraid, because I was naked; and I hid myself."

My count here is forty-six verbs. You'll notice that I counted as a single word any strings of verbs that indicate tense, such as "shall not eat" and "were opened." That's just for clarity. And again, you might do it differently.

GENESIS 3: ADJECTIVES

1 Now the serpent was more crafty than any other wild animal that the LORD God had made. He said to the woman,
"Did God say, 'You shall not eat from any tree in the garden'?" 2 The woman said to the serpent, "We may eat of the
fruit of the trees in the garden; 3 but God said, 'You shall not
eat of the fruit of the tree that is in the middle of the garden,
nor shall you touch it, or you shall die.'" 4 But the serpent
said to the woman, "You will not die; 5 for God knows that
when you eat of it your eyes will be opened, and you will
be like God, knowing good and evil." 6 So when the woman
saw that the tree was good for food, and that it was a delight
to the eyes, and that the tree was to be desired to make one
wise, she took of its fruit and ate; and she also gave some to
her husband, who was with her, and he ate.

7 Then the eyes of both were opened, and they knew
that they were naked; and they sewed fig leaves together
and made loincloths for themselves. 8 They heard the sound
of the LORD God walking in the garden at the time of the
evening breeze, and the man and his wife hid themselves
from the presence of the LORD God among the trees of the
garden. 9 But the LORD God called to the man, and said to
him, "Where are you?" 10 He said, "I heard the sound of you
in the garden, and I was afraid, because I was naked; and I
hid myself."

My count is seven adjectives. You'll notice that I didn't count "good" and "evil" in verse 5 as adjectives; in my reading of the text, they function here as nouns. In verse 6, on the other hand, "good" functions as an adjective, so that's how I counted it. You'll also notice that I counted adjectives and their modifiers—"more crafty"—as one word. You might do the same, or not.

APPENDIX 3

Encountering

An Example of a Reading in Progress

If you'd like to see what reading the verbs might look like in the repertory church as a group works its way through our Genesis 3 text, here's one example. Imagine that the group is considering the verbs in each verse, asking questions drawn from Chapter 3. As they read each verb, they start to chime in with very brief, unfiltered impressions about what they're hearing. They don't worry too much about whether those comments will lead anywhere yet; they know the script in Scripture will present itself as the reading progresses. But notice how reading the verbs focuses the group. They have clear direction and open air. They can rehearse the text with freedom and precision, and they need both.

I won't try to recreate all the group dialogue; that would fill another book and require the services of a court stenographer. But this will give you an idea of the kind of conversation that emerges when a group encounters Scripture in this way. Watch how the questions spark the encounter.

The group goes verse by verse. For each one, it selects different questions to respond to.

GENESIS 3

[1] Now the serpent was more crafty than any other wild animal that the LORD God had made. He said to the woman, "Did God say, 'You shall not eat from any tree in the garden'?"

Who gets what verbs?

- The serpent: "was" and "said."
- God: "had made" and (according to the serpent) "did say . . . shall not eat."

What do the verb tenses and moods tell you?

- "Was" is a form of "to be," which is the reflexive verb. It means the two things on either side of it are equal: the serpent = crafty. (More crafty, actually.)
- "Said": past tense. The serpent is asking the woman whether God has already said this.
- "Shall not" is in the future tense: You can't do this now, or ever! It's also an imperative: God is not negotiating.

What do the verbs stir or evoke in you? What do you remember from the times you or others have played them?

- I told my children, when they were little, what they could and couldn't eat. Sometimes it was a life-and-death situation: *You can't eat that poisonous plant.* Sometimes it was a nutrition issue: *You can't eat candy every single day.* Sometimes it was about table manners: *You can't just grab the last piece of bacon without asking if anyone else would like some, too.*
- When I'm on a diet, the things I know I "shall not eat" are the very things I crave!

» It's such a sneaky thing for the serpent to do—to misquote God and feign innocence.

If you run these verbs through your biblical echo chamber, what do you hear?

» "Did God say . . . ?" It reminds me of Genesis 1. "God said" comes up rather a lot in that first chapter of the Bible. ("God said, 'Let there be light,'" and so on.) There, it was a creating verb; God says it, and it is. Here, the creatures are trying to recall what God said. It's a clarifying verb.

» The "shall nots" are a centerpiece in the Ten Commandments. Which is probably why I have a slight recoil when I hear the phrase.

» I think the rest of the world looks at the church and sees nothing but a lot of people yelling "shall not!" about anything and everything.

If God is a character in this verse, how are God's verbs different from the others?

» God is really at the top of the food chain here. God gets to make, and God gets to give commands—very "in charge" verbs. When everyone quotes you, you're big.

» But God is in the background at this point in the story. They're just talking about God—what God did, what God said. Whatever verbs God has are verbs they *say* God has.

Do any of the verbs surprise you? Why? What were you expecting?

» Well, the snake is talking. . . .

» I'm wondering why God would ever make a very crafty serpent. That seems like a serious error, like inventing the atom bomb.

- The snake's question makes me wonder: Were the human beings the only ones who got the instructions about what to eat and what not to eat? Were the animals left out? Was this a restriction or test God intended only for the human beings?
- The snake's question makes *me* wonder if it has already tried the fruit (snakes are carnivores, right?).

Are there any adjectives in this verse?

- Two: "crafty" and "wild." The serpent gets both. The animals share "wild."
- "Crafty" is the opposite of "wise," which is going to come up later. I'm not sure crafty is a compliment, unless you're a knitter, or trying to think of a way out of trouble.
- "Wild" belongs to the other animals God made. The garden is apparently a jungle. Or an episode of "Wild Kingdom."

> 2 The woman said to the serpent, "We may eat of the fruit of the trees in the garden . . ."

Who gets what verbs?

- The woman: "said."
- The woman and man: "may eat."

What do the verb tenses and moods tell you?

- "May eat" is present tense and ongoing. They are most definitely allowed to eat.

What do the verbs stir or evoke in you? What do you remember from the times you or others have played them?

» The woman is correcting the serpent. She knows the rules better than the serpent (or better than the serpent pretends to know them). She knows that they *are* allowed to eat the fruit of the trees in the garden.

» I was always the one who knew the rules in my family; my brothers and sisters didn't (or pretended they didn't). Which left me in the role of the one who had to quote the rules to them when they were breaking them. Otherwise, our parents would look to me like it was my fault!

» Haven't you ever had the friend who knew the rules inside and out—and all the ways to get around them? And tried to get you to join in? And made fun of you if you wouldn't? Or if you quoted the rules, like the woman does here?

» This really is such a setup. The serpent knows exactly what it's doing: getting the woman to recite the rules so it can tell her how to break them.

And what about those nouns?

» "Fruit" is new. The woman introduces that word.

» Fruit is perishable and seasonal. Does this tree keep on producing forbidden fruit all year? Does the fruit just rot and drop off the tree when no one eats it? Are there safe periods when the tree isn't producing, and you can go near it without a care in the world?

» There really are trees that produce poisonous fruit—and berries. And you better know about them when you're in the woods. Remember *The Hunger Games*?

> 3 ". . . but God said, 'You shall not eat of the fruit of the tree that is in the middle of the garden, nor shall you touch it, or you shall die.'"

Who gets what verbs?

- » God (according to the woman): "said."
- » The woman and man: "shall not eat," "shall not touch," "shall die."

What's the order of those verbs?

- » Eat, touch, die. You do the first two, and you're toast.

What do the verb tenses and moods tell you?

- » Future tense: You can't do this now or ever. And an imperative: No eating or touching that fruit!

What do the verbs stir or evoke in you? What do you remember from the times you or others have played them?

- » The woman adds "touching" to "eating." Whatever this fruit is in the middle of the garden, it's lethal to touch as well as to ingest.
- » The woman doesn't seem unhappy or resentful about the rules at all. She focuses on what they *can* do before she turns to what they *can't*. Very straightforward.
- » If this were a courtroom, we'd call this hearsay. No direct testimony from God; everybody quoting their memory of what God said. That makes me nervous. Memories aren't always reliable.

Are these verbs associated with certain groups or persons? Are they used to stereotype or make broad generalizations?

- » Once again, "shall not eat or touch" makes me think of the

commands adults give to young children for their own safety. Like not touching a hot stove. Or Daddy's computer.
- » "Shall not touch" makes me think of the rules that cultures have about touching women—which is a bit ironic here, since the *woman* is telling the *snake* about those rules.

If God is a character in this verse, how are God's verbs different from the others?
- » God is still giving commands. The woman and man can repeat them, verbatim.
- » But it's still their *memory* of what God said! God hasn't appeared yet.

And what about those nouns?
- » I'm wondering about why the tree is in the "middle" of the garden. The thing that is most off-limits is right at the center of their garden home.
- » If there's a middle, it implies that the garden has a definite shape: boundaries, edges, and limits. But the edgy stuff isn't at the edges here. It's in the middle.

4 But the serpent said to the woman, "You will not die;"

Who gets what verbs?
- » The serpent: "said."
- » The woman (according to the serpent): "will not die."

Do any of the verbs surprise you? Why? What were you expecting?
- » The serpent is contradicting God!

5 ". . . for God knows that when you eat of it your eyes will be opened, and you will be like God, knowing good and evil."

Who gets what verbs?

» God (according to the serpent): "knows."

» The woman and man (according to the serpent): "eat," "will be opened" (their eyes), "will be (like God)," "knowing (good and evil)."

What's the order of those verbs?

» It's a domino sequence: as soon as you eat, your eyes are opened, and you'll be just like God: you'll know good and evil.

What do the verb tenses and moods tell you?

» God knows in two tenses: now and ongoing. As for the human beings' verbs, they're all out in the future, just waiting for them to make it happen!

Do the verbs stir or evoke something in you? What do you remember from the times you or others have played them?

» What does it mean to "know" good and evil? I think I know both. I hope my kids don't.

» I hope my kids know the *difference* between good and evil. But I don't want them to have firsthand knowledge of what evil is and does.

» And I certainly don't want them to learn good and evil from the snake! That's like learning ethics from Darth Vader. Or Hitler.

» Maybe God is the only one who really knows the full extent of good and evil—and can bear to know.

If God is a character in this verse, how are God's verbs different from the others?

- » "Knows" and "knowing" are good verbs for God. I'm relieved God has both.
- » I'm not surprised that none of the other creatures share God's verb. Isn't that what we say?—"God only knows why such-and-such happened. . . ."

And what about those nouns?

- » "Good" and "evil" are nouns here. They exist. They're real.

> [6] So when the woman saw that the tree was good for food, and that it was a delight to the eyes, and that the tree was to be desired to make one wise, she took of its fruit and ate; and she also gave some to her husband, who was with her, and he ate.

Who gets what verbs?

- » The woman: "saw," "took," "ate," "gave."
- » The tree: "was" (good for food, a delight to the eyes) and "to be desired" to "make" one wise.
- » The man: "ate."

What's the order of those verbs?

- » She saw, she took, she ate, she gave. He just ate.

What do the verbs stir or evoke in you? What do you remember from the times you or others have played them?

- » I notice she shared right away. Isn't that what we do—share our food? I also notice he ate what she gave him without objection. Although, presumably, both of these two knew the rules.

- If there was a dialogue between the man and the woman, it isn't reported. That's interesting, since the story up to this point has *only* been dialogue. Why would the narrator leave that out?

Are these verbs associated with certain groups or persons? Are they used to stereotype or make broad generalizations?

- Well, let's just say that centuries of doctrine have attributed all manner of things to women based on this verse. It's a lightning rod for strong opinions.
- It's a lightning rod for theologies that exclude!

If you run these verbs through your biblical echo chamber, what do you hear?

- She saw that it was good. Just like God in Genesis 1: "And God saw that it was good."
- She took the food and gave it to him, and he ate. . . . Do I have to say it?!? Doesn't this sound to anyone else like the words we hear at communion? "Jesus took the bread and broke it and gave it to them, saying, 'Take, eat . . .'" Yikes!

Are there any adjectives in this verse?

- The tree gets two big adjectives. It's "good" (Genesis 1 again) and it makes one "wise," which is different than "crafty." It's the opposite of crafty!
- Wisdom is a huge theme in Scripture. It's a metaphor for God. We're all supposed to desire wisdom, like it says in Ecclesiastes and Proverbs.

- » Wisdom isn't the same as knowledge or intellect or street smarts. It's beyond those. It's a knowledge that knows how to *handle* knowledge for the good of the world.
- » There are only a few people in my life whom I'd call "wise." I've always yearned to be one of them.

And what about those nouns?

- » The tree—which is delicious, delightful, and desirable. It's certainly made to look like everything you could ever want to taste, see, have, or hold.
- » For one noun, it has to carry a slew of verbs and adjectives—maybe more than one noun can reasonably hold. Can a tree feel pressure?

> [7]Then the eyes of both were opened, and they knew that they were naked; and they sewed fig leaves together and made loincloths for themselves.

Who gets what verbs?

- » Their eyes: "were opened."
- » The man and woman: "knew," "sewed," "made."

What's the order of those verbs?

- » You can't know until your eyes are opened. And then you get really busy with the needle and thread.

What do the verb tenses and moods tell you?

- » They didn't open those eyes themselves; "were opened" is passive tense.

Do the verbs stir or evoke something in you? What do you remember from the times you or others have played them?

» I'm the only one in my house who knows how to sew. My partner can't sew on a button. *I'd* be the one sewing those fig leaves.

» I'm impressed, frankly, that "sewing" seems to be a verb everybody knew how to do at the beginning of creation! Good foresight on God's part.

» I can't wait to tell my partner that the Fall of Man is the reason he can't sew.

Do any of the verbs surprise you? Why? What were you expecting?

» "Sewing" doesn't seem to match its noun (fig leaves), to put it mildly.

Are there any adjectives in this verse?

» The woman and man are "naked," and they know it. It's not the adjective they were hoping for (wise).

And what about those nouns?

» Fig leaves?! I guess you grab the first thing you can reach.

» Loincloths?! I guess you cover just the parts you find most embarrassing.

> [8] They heard the sound of the LORD God walking in the garden at the time of the evening breeze, and the man and his wife hid themselves from the presence of the LORD God among the trees of the garden.

Who gets what verbs?

- » The woman and man: "heard," "hid."
- » The Lord God: "walking."

What's the order of those verbs?

- » As soon as you hear those footsteps, you hide!

Do the verbs stir or evoke something in you? What do you remember from the times you or others have played them?

- » I vividly remember hiding from the sound of certain footsteps. It wasn't always as part of a game, either.
- » When I sit in my office, I know immediately who's walking down the hall by the sound of their footsteps. It's the same at home, for that matter. We all have such distinct ways of walking—immediately recognizable.
- » It can be scary hiding outside, in a forest of trees, when night is coming.

If God is a character in this verse, how are God's verbs different from the others?

- » God gets to walk around here. God takes a human verb, you could say; it makes God sound so present, so recognizable.
- » I wonder what the sound of God walking is?

Do any of the verbs surprise you? Why? What were you expecting?

- » Hiding from God would seem to be impossible in every conceivable sense. Points for trying, I guess.

And what about those nouns?

- » "The time of the evening breeze" is such a lovely phrase. The garden is a beautiful and tranquil place here—a paradise. I want to flop down in a hammock and listen to the birds.

» But the evening breeze means night is coming.

[9] But the LORD God called to the man, and said to him, "Where are you?"

Who gets what verbs?

» The LORD God: "called," "said."

» The man (as asked by God): "are" (as in "Where the heck?").

If you run these verbs through your biblical echo chamber, what do you hear?

» "Called" is a verb associated with prophets. God called Moses. Jesus called the disciples.

What do the verbs stir or evoke in you? What do you remember from the times you or others have played them?

» I can hear the voices of my parents ("Where are you?"), calling me in to dinner, and the voices of children playing hide-and-seek.

» When very small children hide, this is what we say, while looking, to delight them. Or while pretending to look; usually, you can see exactly where they are!

» I have a visceral reaction to this scene. Human beings doing their best to hide, and God calling them to come out.

» God must know where we are—but God asks us to *name* where we are. And that is very hard to do.

If God is a character in this verse, how are God's verbs different from the others?

- » God calls. God wants to know where the man is. Does God really not know? Is this a children's game? I'm relieved God is calling, either way.
- » Why is God only calling the man? It's a little disturbing that the woman suddenly drops out of the picture.
- » It seems like that in life sometimes: that God calls some, but not others. And then we get all kinds of explanations for why that is—the elect, the chosen, the promised, the good. This verb makes me very uneasy.

> 10 He said, "I heard the sound of you in the garden, and I was afraid, because I was naked; and I hid myself."

Who gets what verbs?

- » The man: "heard," "was (afraid)," "was (naked)," "hid."

What's the order of those verbs?

- » He heard God, and, after assessing his adjectives, he hid. His report matches the account in verse 8.

What do the verb tenses and moods tell you?

- » Past tense, completed actions. At least he's owning his verbs. And speaking them aloud.
- » Yes, but did you notice he's only owning half of his verbs from the previous verses?!

What do the verbs stir or evoke in you? What do you remember from the times you or others have played it?

- » These are hard confessions to make out loud. Whenever our adjectives are "naked" and "afraid," it's excruciating to *say* anything, let alone confess that you *heard* and *hid*.
- » Our prayers of confession contain versions of this verse. I wonder what it might be like to reclaim the language here, in its raw state.
- » One of my recurring nightmares is that I'm naked and afraid—literally. And can't find my clothes or my way.

Are there any adjectives in this verse?

- » Two big ones: the man is "afraid" and "naked." Or afraid because he's naked; the second adjective triggers the first. It strikes me that fear is the trigger for so many of our worst verbs.

APPENDIX 4

Speaking

A Group Process for Asking the Six Questions

This is the process I use for working with the six questions in repertory church groups. I print out copies of the questions for each person. But don't rely on writing down your responses and reading them from your sheets! Challenge yourself and your group to do the exercise orally, and together.

This process is designed for two persons to do together.

After your group has finished reading the verbs and rehearsing your text, divide into pairs.

Have each pair turn their chairs to face one another, and take turns asking each other the six questions below.

Each pair should speak directly to one another and make eye contact, looking right at each other.

1. *What's the place in the text that gets you?*—that is, fascinates you, bothers you, troubles you, thrills you, haunts you, angers you, gladdens you, or otherwise jumps up to meet you? The place in the text that sticks to you, no matter how hard you try to shake it off, is the script the text is offering you, and the moment of

encounter you must pay attention to. It contains the seed of what you'll say. Locate the place and name the verse.

2. *Why does it get you?*—or fascinate you, bother you, trouble you, thrill you, haunt you, anger you, gladden you, or otherwise jump up to meet you? This is for you to name for yourself: how this text has become your script. You don't have to tell anyone, but you do have to know. Be honest.
3. *From this moment in the text that gets you, what do you know about God?* Now change the subject back to God. What do you know and believe about God from playing this script? State this in response to what the text has shown you—or not shown you. For instance, the text may have lifted up the goodness and greatness of God's verbs: something you want to reaffirm. Or it might have pointed out that God was absent and silent here: something you want to question, counter, or lament.
4. *Why does your community need to hear this today—what you know about God? Why is it important to tell them?* Now move to your community. Why is it important for them to hear this—what you know about God, and God's verbs, from what you've seen in this text—today, right now? Why does the script matter for them? Or think of it this way: What you want to say is a gift you offer your community. What do you want to give them right now? What does this script in Scripture offer them that the world's scripts don't?
5. *What do you want to say?* This is the focus or main idea, the summary of your encounter with the text that you want to share with your community. It's the script you want to give them. Say it in one sentence, if you can. Begin like this: "[Name of partner], here's what I want to say to you: [. . . .]."
6. *What do you hope these words will do?* This is the function or

stated intention of the script you want to give them. It's what you hope will happen. Say it in one sentence, if you can. Begin like this: "[Name of partner], here's what I hope these words will do: [. . . .]."

Allow 10–15 minutes or so for this process. Then have the pairs reform as a group. Those who are willing may share their responses to the six questions or summarize them.

Alternatively, each pair that is willing can re-enact their experience for the group by turning their chairs to face one another as the convener prompts them and the group vocally encourages them ("You're doing great–keep going!"). This can be very helpful if the text was difficult or the group feels stuck; a pair can ask the larger group for feedback as it works through the six questions.

And remember: cheering one another on is important! Responding to these questions isn't easy to do when others are watching and listening to answers that may not be easy to give.

If you want to have a record of your group's scriptural encounter and the myriad ways in which you "saw something true" from the same text, one person might volunteer to take notes and start a folder. This is remarkable wisdom to return to down the road.

APPENDIX 5

Sharing

An Example of the Six Questions in Progress

When it's time to move toward speaking in the repertory church, everyone is invited to *say something true* about what they've seen and heard in the text—and you can count on being amazed at how moving, challenging, and different those responses will be. If you'd like to see how the process might play out in one group, here are six examples of people working through the six questions from Chapter 6. (I know—that's a lot of sixes!)

Imagine that, once again, the group has been reading the same text of Genesis 3:1–10. They are in fine fettle: the sail went well, the group let loose, the wild things were out, and the verbs were hopping. The scripts in Scripture appeared right on schedule, and the wolf suits this week were especially handsome. As the group shifts to the next phase of its time together, settling down to reflect on what it's experienced, they divide into pairs to ask each other the six questions. After ten minutes or so, they come back to the circle and regroup. The convener asks, "Would anyone like to share their responses—to *say something true* about the Scripture we've encountered together?"

Some prefer to be quiet at this time, keeping the experience to themselves a little longer, and that's fine. Six others agree to share with the whole group. They begin with the verses that caught their attention in the reading, and then describe how they worked through the six questions.

First Example

". . . the tree was to be desired to make one wise. . . ."

1. *What's the place in the text that gets you?* Verse 6: "So when the woman saw that the tree was good for food, and that it was a delight to the eyes, and that the tree was to be desired to make one wise, she took of its fruit and ate; and she also gave some to her husband, who was with her, and he ate."
2. *Why does it get you?* I have teenagers. Last summer, one of their friends died from a heroin overdose. This boy started out desiring what we all do: more life, more experience, more beauty and delight. Maybe he even wanted wisdom, or the teenage equivalent of that. But he met a crafty snake peddling shiny fruit that took him down. Why are we so easily tricked, as human beings, into believing that whatever a snake offers us will make us wise? Adolescence has always been hard, but these days, it's terrifying.
3. *From this place in the text that gets you, what do you know about God?* I know God is the only one who can show us what true wisdom and desire are; whatever the snake is selling, it didn't come from a shelf in God's store. I also know God sets some boundaries for us that are for our own protection, even if we can't see it at the time.

4. *Why does your community need to hear this today—what you know about God?* Our town is reeling from this young man's death. What happened to him could happen to any of our children; in thousands of cases, it already has. Our kids are vulnerable, and we need to tell them that God is real, God loves them, God loves their desire for wisdom and connection, and God is their first and best place to look for it. And because *we* love them, we've set boundaries for them, to urge them to look in the right places for these things.
5. *What do you want to say?* Your desire for wisdom and experience in every facet of life is one of the most beautiful things about you, and God created you for it—so search in the right places, the ones where God has promised to meet you.
6. *What do you hope these words will do?* I hope these words will encourage parents and their kids to talk to one another about where God might be, in all the thirsts and desires of adolescence, and where God might not be—which is definitely where the snakes are going to show up.

Second Example

"Then the eyes of both were opened. . . ."

1. *What's the place in the text that gets you?* Verse 7: "Then the eyes of both were opened, and they knew that they were naked. . . ."
2. *Why does it get you?* I'm thinking about how hard it is for us to open our eyes to painful truths about ourselves. We can't seem to do it on our own. It's like something has to break first—or break down. Or break apart. Why does it take a crisis for us to

look at our own brokenness and finally see it for what it is? Yet once we see everything laid bare, could the possibility of change be a hidden gift?

3. *From this place in the text that gets you, what do you know about God?* I know that in the light of God's truth, there's hope for healing and reconciliation and real growth. Even in the most painful moments of epiphany, God can move with liberating power.
4. *Why does your community need to hear this today—what you know about God?* We're trying to talk openly about racism and white privilege in our diverse community. The "Black Lives Matter" movement is prompting us to take our conversation to a new level of honesty, and we're holding more open forums and discussions. It's hard work. The white people in our community say they want to listen to what the people of color have to say, but when it gets too painful, they shut down. It's like even their pain takes privilege! We don't want to give up on our commitment to talk, but this "their eyes were opened" phase is exhausting. We need to know that God's a part of it and can move us through it, so we don't bog down in despair.
5. *What do you want to say?* Even in the most painful eye-opening moments, when we're learning and saying hard truths that strip us bare, God is moving with liberating power to make us into the Beloved Community that Dr. King dreamed of.
6. *What do you hope these words will do?* I hope these words will strengthen and embolden each of us to keep talking and listening to one another through the pain.

Third Example

". . . they sewed fig leaves together. . . ."

1. *What's the place in the text that gets you?* Verse 7: ". . . they sewed fig leaves together and made loincloths for themselves."
2. *Why does it get you?* I can picture them, sewing feverishly, with whatever they could grab that was close at hand. And I can picture how feeble and lame the results were. It makes me think of the lengths we'll go to to cover the things we're ashamed of—and how those things don't work in the long run. And how we all pretend that they do. I see a lot of that honor-shame dynamic in my community.
3. *From this place in the text that gets you, what do you know about God?* I know God calls us to drop the cover-ups and let go of the shame, so we can walk in the light of truth and justice.
4. *Why does your community need to hear this today—what you know about God?* Domestic violence is a real issue in my community. We're trying to educate on every level—schools, workplaces, social services, police—in order to stop the violence, support the victims, and hold perpetrators accountable. This story can help us address the role shame plays when women get the message that their abuse is too shameful to report, and we as a community cover up the problem. We need to hear God's call to come into the light.
5. *What do you want to say?* We can take on the issue of domestic violence in our community by promising one another that we will trade our fig leaves for the light of God.
6. *What do you hope these words will do?* I hope these words will

empower us to take up the honorable work of dismantling domestic violence in our community, from the roots up.

Fourth Example

"They heard the sound of the LORD God walking in the garden. . . ."

1. *What's the place in the text that gets you?* Verse 8: "They heard the sound of the LORD God walking in the garden at the time of the evening breeze. . . ."
2. *Why does it get you?* I haven't heard the sound of God for so long. Maybe I did, once; now, most of what I hear is silence. But I'd give a lot to hear that sound again. Just to know God exists, and is out there, moving among us, like one of us. The sound of God knocking on my door would be awesome, but I'd settle for the sound of God walking around outside, nearby, in the cool of the evening.
3. *From this place in the text that gets you, what do you know about God?* I know that God is always with us. Even when we don't hear God, God is there, and moving.
4. *Why does your community need to hear this today—what you know about God?* A lot of people are dealing with grief in our community; we've had more than our share of deaths. That grief is like a thick cloud of silence. It really isolates us from one another, and keeps us from believing that God is out there at all. We need assurance that God is, and that if we listen, we'll hear God moving, however faintly.
5. *What do you want to say?* You may not hear it now, but God

is walking in a garden you know, at the time of the evening breeze, and God will keep walking nearby you until you can hear those footsteps again.

6. *What do you hope these words will do?* I hope these words will offer hopeful and honest comfort to those who are grieving: yes, you will hear God again; and yes, it will take time.

Fifth Example

"But the LORD God called to the man, and said to him, 'Where are you?'"

1. *What's the place in the text that gets you?* Verse 9: "But the LORD God called to the man, and said to him, 'Where are you?'"
2. *Why does it get you?* For a few years now, I've been wondering if God is calling me into ministry. It's not like an angel landed in my living room with a hand-written letter from Jesus. It's more like a constant refrain that keeps coming back. I've ignored it so far—I have a job I like, a life I've planned—but I think I'm starting to hide from that call, hide from God, like the man and the woman in this story. I wonder if the message has shifted from "I want you" to "Where *are* you?!"
3. *From this place in the text that gets you, what do you know about God?* I know God calls human beings to do God's work in the world. I know God keeps calling until we answer.
4. *Why does your community need to hear this today—what you know about God?* I don't think I'm the only one who's experiencing this. It's difficult to decipher if God's call to us is real, let alone what it actually is. Our community is in a discernment period,

trying to decide whether we're going to get involved in an outreach ministry that's happening in our neighborhood. Some of us don't think it's a good time for it, or that it's even our responsibility to get involved. I wonder if we all need to hear more about the ways God calls us into ministry—which may include coming out of hiding to do it.

5. *What do you want to say?* God's call to us isn't only to *do* and to *go*; it is also a repeated call for us to come out from where we may be hiding in fear and denial.
6. *What do you hope these words will do?* I hope these words will summon us to serious reflection and self-inventory, on both a personal and a communal level: Is God calling, and are we hiding?

Sixth Example

"... I was afraid, because I was naked, and I hid myself. . . ."

1. *What's the place in the text that gets you?* Verse 10: "He said, 'I heard the sound of you in the garden, and I was afraid, because I was naked, and I hid myself. . . .'"
2. *Why does it get you?* I can't believe how honest the man's confession is. He could have just raised his hand and said, "I'm here," and left it at that. Instead, he told God why he was hiding in the first place; he actually admitted he was naked and afraid. I don't think I've been that open with God before. Maybe that's why my prayers feel so awkward and stilted. If I was that honest with God, would it take me to a deeper place spiritually?
3. *From this place in the text that gets you, what do you know about*

God? I know God is the one calling us to be that open. God is listening. Maybe God even expects that kind of honesty from us: not to simply admit our mistakes, but to name the nakedness and fear behind them.

4. *Why does your community need to hear this today—what you know about God?* A lot of us are interested in prayer. We're looking for ways to come out from wherever we're hiding and engage in some spiritual practices that will draw us closer to God and one another. We've been collecting stories from Scripture to use in meditation, but we never thought to read this one. For many of us, it has such negative associations—a lot of old tapes we've heard before about original sin, women's disobedience, and gullible females. But maybe there are other ways to read it. Maybe we need to hear about God's call to come out and confess the nakedness and fear behind our brokenness.
5. *What do you want to say?* God calls us to complete honesty, to tell God of all the places we're hiding because of our nakedness and fear.
6. *What do you hope these words will do?* I hope these words will invite us into deeper spiritual relationship with God, and encourage us to look for new texts as spiritual resources.